Active Bodies, Active Brains

Building Thinking Skills Through Physical Activity

Mary Ellen Clancy, PhD

University of Tampa

HUMAN KINETICS

Library of Congress Cataloging-in-Publication Data

Clancy, Mary Ellen, 1951-
  Active bodies, active brains : building thinking skills through physical activity / Mary Ellen Clancy.
      p. cm.
  Includes bibliographical references.
  ISBN-13: 978-0-7360-5096-8 (soft cover)
  ISBN-10: 0-7360-5096-5 (soft cover)
  1. Physical education for children. 2. Critical thinking in children. I. Title.
  GV443.C55 2006
  372.86--dc22   2005037755
ISBN-10: 0-7360-5096-5
ISBN-13: 978-0-7360-5096-8

The Web addresses cited in this text were current as of April 6, 2006, unless otherwise noted.

Acquisitions Editor: Bonnie Pettifor; **Developmental Editor:** Jacqueline Eaton Blakley; **Assistant Editor:** Bethany J. Bentley; **Copyeditor:** Bob Replinger; **Proofreader:** Sarah Wiseman; **Permission Manager:** Dalene Reeder; **Graphic Designer:** Nancy Rasmus; **Graphic Artist:** Yvonne Griffith; **Photo Manager:** Sarah Ritz; **Cover Designer:** Keith Blomberg; **Photographer (interior and cover):** Karen L. Shaw; **Art Manager:** Kelly Hendren; **Illustrator:** Keri Evans; **Printer:** Versa Press

Printed in the United States of America   10 9 8 7 6 5 4 3 2 1

Human Kinetics
Web site: www.HumanKinetics.com

United States: Human Kinetics
P.O. Box 5076
Champaign, IL 61825-5076
800-747-4457
e-mail: humank@hkusa.com

Canada: Human Kinetics
475 Devonshire Road Unit 100
Windsor, ON N8Y 2L5
800-465-7301 (in Canada only)
e-mail: orders@hkcanada.com

Europe: Human Kinetics
107 Bradford Road, Stanningley
Leeds LS28 6AT, United Kingdom
+44 (0) 113 255 5665
e-mail: hk@hkeurope.com

Australia: Human Kinetics
57A Price Avenue
Lower Mitcham, South Australia 5062
08 8277 1555
e-mail: liaw@hkaustralia.com

New Zealand: Human Kinetics
Division of Sports Distributors NZ Ltd.
P.O. Box 300 226 Albany
North Shore City
Auckland
0064 9 448 1207
e-mail: info@humankinetics.co.nz

This book is dedicated to my parents, John and Dorothy Clancy, who let me become a physical education teacher instead of a nurse; my children, Caitlin M. and Patrick A.A. Clancy, who helped and hindered and were always a welcome distraction; and my friends and colleagues Penny A. Portman, Sandra L. Van Ardsall, Barbara Hruska, and Sondra Iverson, who kept me focused and sane during this process, and especially Tova R. Rubin, who collaborated with me in my initial research and encouraged me to take on this project in the first place.

CONTENTS

ACTIVITY FINDER

To help you quickly find activities that are suitable for your students, the following table indexes each of the book's activities by several helpful categories. It's also a handy way of quickly locating activities you've used before, as they are listed alphabetically by name.

Key

Intelligence types

L	Linguistic
LM	Logical–mathematical
S	Spatial
K	Bodily–kinesthetic
M	Musical
IE	Interpersonal
IA	Intrapersonal
N	Naturalistic

Academic subjects

 Math

 Language arts

 Science

 Health

 Social studies

 Visual and performing arts

Complexity

 Introductory

 Basic

 Intermediate

 Complex

Activity	NASPE standards	Intelligence types	Academic subjects	Complexity	Page
Adverbs on the Move	1, 2, 6	L, K	[book]	[2 brains]	105
The Announcer	2, 5, 6	L, K, IE	[book] [art]	[2 brains]	88
As the Wind Blows	1, 5, 6	N, K, L	[science]	[2 brains]	74
The Best Meal	1, 5, 6	K, S, IE	[apple]	[3 brains]	136
Bone Volley	1, 2, 5	N, K, IA, IE	[apple]	[2 brains]	82
Category Tag	1, 4, 5	K, S, IE	[apple]	[3 brains]	118
Centipede Challenge	2, 5	IE, K, N	[science]	[3 brains]	130
Circuit Setup	1, 2, 5	IE, K, S, L	[apple]	[4 brains]	163
Clouds of Parachutes	5	N, K, S, IE	[science]	[3 brains]	132
Collection Agency	1, 2, 5	K, IE	[globe]	[3 brains]	126
Compliment Tag	1, 5	L, IE	[apple]	[2 brains]	102
Contribution Fitness	1, 4, 5	K, IE, M	[apple]	[1 brain]	57
Current Events	2, 5, 6	IE, IA, K	[globe]	[4 brains]	170
Digit Dancer	1, 2, 4	S, IE, K	[apple]	[2 brains]	90
Fact or Fiction Fitness	1, 2	K, I, L	[apple]	[1 brain]	65
Figure and Run	1, 5	K, LM, S, IE	[math]	[3 brains]	138
Food Fitness	4, 6	K, S, IE	[apple]	[3 brains]	143
Hoop-to-It Math	1, 2	LM, S, IE, K	[apple] [math]	[3 brains]	133
How I See It	5	K, IE, IA,S	[art]	[3 brains]	120

(continued)

Activity	NASPE standards	Intelligence types	Academic subjects	Complexity	Page
Mural, Mural, on the Wall	1, 2, 5, 6	K, S			80
Music in the House	1, 6	M, IA, K			108
Musical Setup	1, 2, 5	S, M, IE, K			171
Nature Run	1, 5	N, S, IA, K			66
Number Write	1, 5, 6	S, IE, LM			48
Numbers by Body	1, 5, 6	LM, IE, K			50
Obstacles for Learning	1, 4	S, K			112
Paper, Scissors, Stone Tag	1, 5	K, S, IE			76
PE Summary	2	K, L, IA			92
Personal Assessment	2, 3, 4, 6	IA, K, L			152
Personal Pattern Moves	2, 4	LM, S, IE			158
Personal Warm-Up	2, 3, 4, 5	IA, K, LM			150
Play by Play	1, 2, 6	L, IE, IA			86
Read and Move	1, 2, 5, 6	L, IE, K			104
Reorder the Class	2	M, S			103
Robot	1, 2, 5, 6	K, S, IA, IE			164
Roll a Move	1, 5	LM, M, IE			54
Sentence Tag	2, 5	L, K, S			140

(continued)

(continued)

Activity	NASPE standards	Intelligence types	Academic subjects	Complexity	Page
Spelling B-Line	1, 2, 5	L, IE, K			62
Sport Shop	1, 2, 5	K, IE, LM			154
Sport Skills Square Dance	1, 2, 5, 6	M, K, IE, S, L			168
Story Time	1, 2, 5, 6	L, IE, K			46
Stretch Band Shapes	1, 2, 5, 6	S, K, L			84
Stump the Teacher	2, 5	IA, L			100
Survival Too	1, 2, 5	K, LM, S, IE			148
Tag Team Fitness	1, 2, 4	K, S			166
Trex	1, 4, 6	N, K, IA			124
What Are We Doing Today?	2, 5	IA, L			44
Whole-Body Feelings	5, 6	IA, K			52
Word Relay	1, 2, 5	K, L, IE			96

PREFACE

Active Bodies, Active Brains is a guide for physical education and classroom teachers who want to help their students become better movers *and* learners. One of the first of its kind, this book explains the current theories behind the movement–learning connection and offers ready-to-use activities that foster this connection in students.

Cutting-edge educational research is proving that movement and other brain-compatible techniques support the development of thinking skills in students. Learning requires efficient use of the brain to acquire information or memories and then manipulate data to solve predicaments and generate solutions. The purpose of this book is to provide educators with information, processes, and practical activities to support educational goals, particularly in the area of thinking.

This book has been developed from what is currently known and theorized about brain-compatible educational practices, the value of movement in learning, and the development of thinking skills and processes. With this basis, *Active Bodies, Active Brains* offers teaching techniques; a method of developing lessons and curriculum to teach thinking; and specific guidance, examples, and activities to allow teachers to improve students' learning and thinking.

The organization of the content leads you from theory to practice. You'll find the following features, and more:

- An introduction to the theory behind brain-compatible learning
- A discussion of the importance of movement in learning
- Definitions of Gardner's learning frames and specialized thinking processes
- A process of moving toward the development of a thinking curriculum
- Real-world strategies to support thinking and the use of brain-compatible practices
- A method of assessing thinking
- Movement activities designed to support thinking

By the conclusion of chapter 1, you will understand the basics of how the brain functions to learn and how movement can support learning. This information offers a rationale for increasing movement opportunities, for advocating for increased physical education in the schools, and for positively affecting students' learning. Chapter 1 also introduces the basic types of thinking, thinking skills, and specialized thinking processes commonly used in education. Specific brain-compatible techniques and exercises that you can use in your classes are included. Try one or two techniques and see how they improve the learning environment!

Chapter 2 guides you through the process of making yours a thinking curriculum. Included are tips on adjusting your current curriculum to support thinking, developing lessons to teach thinking, and even reconfiguring an entire curriculum. The chapter closes with a section devoted to assessment of thinking in your students.

Chapters 3 through 6 are full of ready-made games and activities that support the development of thinking and physical activity in your students. These activities are easy to adapt and customize; often, they require little or no equipment and can be played using movement skills and concepts of your choice. The specific learning style or frame (based on Gardner's theory of multiple intelligences) is identified to allow you to teach to students' specific type of intelligence. Thinking skills used in the activities are listed. And each activity closes with brain-compatible techniques to incorporate with the teaching of the activity.

The activities are loosely organized by progressive complexity according to the types and processes of thinking needed for completing the tasks, the subject content, and the complexity of the activity itself. These categories are not set in stone, though. Complexity is subjective, so select activities or adapt games to fit the specific goals of your lessons and the developmental levels of your students. And, although guidance is given for the specific thinking skills or processes that could be addressed with each game, you can choose to emphasize any thinking process required to meet the goals of the lesson.

The activities in chapter 3 introduce a single, simple thinking skill into a game structure or lesson content. The basic activities in chapter 4 increase the complexity to encompass more combinations of thinking skills. Intermediate activities, the subject of chapter 5, involve the use of specialized thinking processes and are more group oriented to increase the potential and stimulation for thinking. Finally, chapter 6 is made up of games involving more complicated structures to challenge the students' thinking abilities.

Movement as a means of fostering learning continues to gain support within the educational community. Because physical activity is the main means through which physical educators teach, we must be its best advocates and use it effectively to produce healthy, active, and thinking students.

ACKNOWLEDGMENTS

This book would not have been completed without the advice, patience, and guidance of my editor, Jacqueline Eaton Blakley.

Special thanks to photographer Karen L. Shaw, to physical education specialists Lisa Beamer and Oscar Laboy, and to the children of Villa Madonna School.

HOW TO USE THIS BOOK

Each activity in this book includes a breakdown of its components and skills that will help you choose and customize activities for your students.

> See at a glance which NASPE standards the activity addresses.

Story Time 📖

NASPE Standards

1, 2, 5, 6

> Your students have a range of learning styles according to Gardner's theory of multiple intelligences; this section shows which learners will respond best to the activity.

Intelligence Types

L, IE, K

Thinking Skills

> To help you plan specific thinking skills in your curriculum, each activity lists the thinking skills practiced and taught.

Analysis, synthesis, decision making, elaboration, rela...

Movement Skills

Whatever is necessary for the story, o..., ...assign o...

> Movement skills needed and reinforced in the activity are listed so you can select activities that fit movement skills being taught in a unit.

Equipment

Props may be helpful. Use short books that the stud... or that they could easily read in class.

Formation

> Handy equipment list and description of game setup helps you prepare quickly.

Place small groups of four students a... ...round the gym. Place a short book, photocopies or printo... or a series of pictures at each station.

Description

> Game action is described in easy-to-follow steps.

1. Ask students to take turns read... ...lling a story using the pictures. You may have to cue stude... ...o change reading or telling roles. For example, have each student read a paragraph or a page.

2. Once the story is read or told, ask students to act out the story literally, or to interpret it as they choose, depending on the abilities of the group. For example, an abstract way to act out a story is to ask students to convey the message of the story using just one movement.

3. Place two groups together and let one act out their story while the other group is the audience. Then switch. Rotate groups.

Movement–Learning Connection

> Each activity features tips and techniques for reinforcing the movement—learning connection.

- Before students read the story, ask them to guess what the story is about from its title.

- ...f stress levels rise, break off from the activity and have students stretch ...eep emotions at moderate levels.

- ...group cannot come up with ideas, have them move within the ...mnasium space (or be active in some manner) to increase circulation to their brains. Then have them regroup.

CHAPTER 1

Introduction to Brain-Compatible Instruction

Our marvelously complex brains have long been a mystery. Even with exciting developments in technology, which give us a much clearer picture of what is happening in the brain as we move and think, much remains to be discovered.

The Brain and How It Learns

The brain, essentially a mass of neurons, or nerve cells, is interconnected with other neurons and central nervous system structures. Specialized bundles of nerve cells in the brain serve specific functions. In general, the brain is divided into two hemispheres. Although the two halves usually work as a coordinated unit, the right hemisphere is associated with holistic and intuitive mental processes, whereas the left half deals more with logical processing. The *corpus callosum*, a band of cells that connects the two hemispheres of the brain, helps to integrate the functions of both halves for effective learning.

The brain is also divided into three general areas: the *hindbrain, or brain stem;* the *midbrain;* and the *forebrain, or cerebral cortex.* Figure 1.1 shows the brain and its structures. Specific brain functions can be shared across a variety of brain structures or areas.

The brain stem consists of the *pons*, which controls automatic functions such as breathing; the *medulla oblongata*, a network of neurons

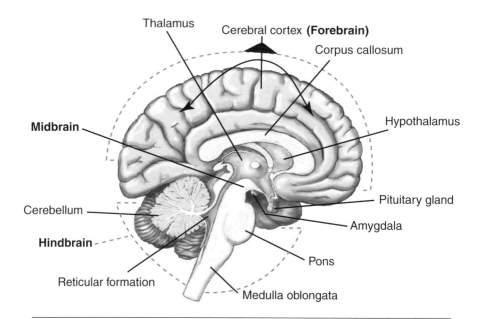

Figure 1.1 Major brain structures.

that receives information to regulate basic life support; the *reticular formation*, which helps control awareness levels; and the *cerebellum*, which stores and regulates movement patterns and is essential for balance, posture, and muscle coordination.

Other significant brain structures include

- the *thalamus*, a relay station that directs the flow of information from the sensory organs and the cerebral cortex;
- the *hypothalamus*, the control center for the regulation of warmth, hunger, and sleep, and the site where stress response is generated;
- the *amygdala*, the control center for emotion;
- the *pituitary gland,* the "master" gland of the endocrine system that controls the functions of the other endocrine glands; and
- the *cerebral cortex*, which is involved in many complex brain functions, including memory, attention, perceptual awareness, thinking, language, and consciousness.

The first step that the brain takes in learning and in storing memories is to interpret sensory information. Any data received through the senses is encoded, and the sensory areas (for example, the *visual cortex)* of the brain attempt to match the pattern of the sensory input with patterns already stored in neural pathways. If a pattern does not emerge or if further conscious attention is not paid to these perceptions, the sensory input is disregarded. But if a pattern is recognized or the sensory data do capture the attention of the brain, the person becomes consciously aware of it and the brain stores it for a longer period in what is called *working memory,* or *short-term memory.* The function of working memory is to connect new perceptions with previously learned information—that is, memories. Because of its limited storage capacity, working memory can retain information for only 15 to 20 seconds (Hannaford 1995; Jensen 1998b; Wolfe 2001).

When new sensory perceptions are associated with patterns of previously stored information or further conscious attention is paid to the stimuli, the perception moves from working memory into *long-term memory.* Long-term memory allows us to recall what we have experienced in the past if we have processed or practiced that experience a sufficient number of times. Although memories remain in long-term storage indefinitely, if not called upon or used, the means to access and assemble them declines (Hannaford 1995; Wolfe 2001). Long-term memories are necessary to allow the frontal lobes of the brain access to essential information and procedures needed for higher-order thinking or movement. Throughout life, the brain constantly reorganizes neural connections to allow access to memories that it needs to meet the demands placed on it (Jensen 1998a, b).

The cerebellum plays an important role in producing a motor act as it works in concert with the motor cortex. The cerebellum assembles the necessary information and calculates the sequence and contributions of muscle contractions required for producing the desired movement. After sending the impulses to the respective muscles, the cerebellum monitors the ensuing response to ensure smooth execution of the motor plan while also monitoring bodily balance and posture (Jensen 1998b; Wolfe 2001). Interestingly, more neural pathways go from the cerebellum to areas on the cortex of the brain associated with cognition and thinking than lead from the cortex to the cerebellum (Hannaford 1995).

The Movement-Learning Connection

Physical education is a terrific laboratory not only for improving students' fitness but also for building their brainpower. As we learn more about the connection between movement and learning, we discover more teaching opportunities that exploit this connection. In this section we explore some ways that movement enhances learning and introduce specific teaching techniques that you can use in the physical education classroom to help your students be better movers *and* better learners.

Movement Builds a Better Brain

Humans must move to develop and maintain neural networks or memories. Soon after the brain begins to form in utero, synapses (the connections between individual brain cells) begin firing to lay down a blueprint of how the brain will be wired. Children raised in active, stimulating environments produce more and denser neural connections (Bruer 1991; Nash 1997). Starting at around age 10, synaptic connections that are not needed or not used are eliminated or pruned (Diamond and Hopson 1998; Nash 1997). Neural networks that are used are reinforced and strengthened. This process of reorganization of neural pathways according to the demands placed on the brain continues throughout the life span (Jensen 1998a, b). In addition, when the body is inactive for 20 minutes or longer, the ability of the neurons to communicate with each other declines (Kinoshita 1997).

The cerebellum, prominent in maintaining balance, posture, and muscle coordination, is now thought to play an expanded role in memory, emotion, language, decision making, spatial perception, and nonverbal cueing (Wolfe 2001). The cerebellum may function to filter and integrate memories and sensory information to support complex decision making (Jensen 1998b). When connected to movement, cognitive information is more easily remembered and recalled (Hannaford 1995; Jensen

1998b). The link between movement and cognition in the cerebellum implies that physical education activities have value in boosting learning (Blakemore 2003). Exercising the actions of the cerebellum through movement strengthens neural pathways leading to the cognitive areas of the brain.

You can encourage the brain-building power of movement in your physical education classroom in specific ways.

1. **Build in time for processing.** To acquire memories, students need assistance and adequate time to encode sensory information, recognize patterns, assemble memories, and interpret them as part of the instructional process (Johnson 1997). You can encourage use of processing time by pausing to think when students ask a complex question and by waiting five seconds before responding or selecting a respondent. After instruction, give students time to assemble memories before they move.

2. **Use memories of similar situations to allow students a base on which to build a new memory** (Jensen 1998b). Always review what you taught in the previous class. Ask students to identify or discover similar or related knowledge or movements before or while presenting new information (e.g., "What does this remind you of? When did we do this before?"). Recall past activities similar to the new one.

3. **Give previews of what is to come.** After offering clues, have students guess what the lesson will include that day or what activities you will present. Insert a minilesson on an upcoming lesson or unit. Post information in the instructional space about the next unit or event (Jensen 1998a).

4. **Help students recognize patterns of neural input to form a perception.** Have students tell or show what was similar or different from previously learned movement activities. Tell students what pattern to look for in a class and then identify it whenever it occurs. Ask, "When you see this, what should you do? What will happen next?"

5. **Link the parts to the whole and the whole to the parts.** Demonstrate the whole game, move, or routine and then ask students to identify parts that they need to refine or clarify. Link specific content to the big picture (e.g., "We need to learn this so that we can play better"). Present segments and then have students put it together or in order (Jensen 1998a).

6. **Organize information into chunks.** To organize large amounts of information, students need help assembling *chunks,* or *frames* (Perkins 1986), which are meaningful units of information that

they can expand with experience or link to other chunks of memory. Use visuals, diagrams, or graphic organizers to organize information. Allow props, but wean students off them when proficiency increases. Draw a sun diagram (circle in the center with line radiating out from it) and then have students develop suggestions for each ray to guide a discussion. Have students develop movement songs, stories, analogies, acronyms, or poems. Substitute exercise descriptions for traditional verses in songs. For example, have students sing "If you're fit and you show it, jump up high" to the tune of "If You're Happy and You Know It."

7. **Use movement routines to help students remember information.** Assign a term or concept to each move of a routine and have students practice them together. Students can act out concepts to a peer who must identify the concepts. Link movement acronyms, songs, poems, or stories with information. For example, you could tie the components of fitness to the following movements:

- Muscular strength (mimic an overhead press)
- Muscular endurance (jump in place 10 times)
- Flexibility (stretch triceps muscles)
- Cardiorespiratory fitness (run in place for 30 seconds)
- Body composition (bodybuilder pose)

8. **Provide multiple opportunities for practice.** Because memories and the pathways to them will fade if not used, remember to provide multiple opportunities to practice and review (Jensen 1998a). Repeat a move one more time. Review previously learned skills. Vary the practice conditions to keep students' attention. Have students explore where they might use a particular skill or concept in their lives outside school.

9. **Revisit previously learned concepts or activities often.** For warm-up, have students play a game or perform a routine that they learned earlier in the school year and then add a new twist. After a unit is long over, ask students to recall key elements that you taught. Play a never-ending quiz show game "Stump the Student," in which you ask students questions about previously learned content. Alternatively, play "Stump the Teacher" by having students form questions.

Movement Encourages Holistic Learning

The brain functions and learns as a unified whole to produce thought and movement (Hannaford 1995). As neural pathways for early memories are formed, the cognitive, emotional, and motor experiences are laid as one, forming an interconnected neural highway for that memory (Piaget 1963; Buschner 1990). When you use a whole-brain approach to learning, students can access learned information through any of the "routes" (e.g., cognitive, motor). Because the brain craves novelty, stimulation, and change, adding movement to learning, altering the method of presentation (e.g., verbal to visual), or adding something novel to the learning setting wakes up the brain as it reorients itself to the change and returns to more holistic function (Hannaford 1995; Promislow 1999).

How can you keep your physical education students on their toes, physically and mentally?

1. **Present new or complex information by addressing one sensory modality at a time.** Talk when it is quiet. Talk without demonstration and then demonstrate without talking. Don't ask students to read and listen at the same time. For example, don't use overhead slides while lecturing; reading the slides can distract students from listening.

2. **Strive to surprise the brain.** Change should be constant. Vary the space, speed, instructor (for example, use peer teaching), rules, groups, equipment, and so on when students' attention lags or when they have accomplished the movement goal. Do something unexpected. Have "last to first" days in which the class progresses from the end to beginning. Have a day off during which you review previously learned content.

3. **Vary the manner in which you present content.** Use peer teaching, video, cooperative learning, guest teachers, task cards, technology, or group work as a means to present information. Change the location from which you deliver instruction. Change instructional spaces often. Change the positions that children assume as they learn (e.g., stand, sit, lie) (Jensen 2000).

4. **Perform movements designed to focus and help the brain work as an integrated whole.** Use contralateral or crossing-the-midline activities (see discussion on page 11). Develop students' fitness levels to improve the efficiency of brain function. Use relaxation exercises to quiet stress and open the brain for learning. Have students perform the skill in slow motion while focusing on a body part and then have them perform at game speed.

5. **Learn your students' *cycles of engagement*** (Jensen 1998b). When students start to hit a lull or dull period, change the task or activity. Present complex or novel information when students are most alert. Be mindful of the time of day that the class meets and adjust as necessary. For example, if students are sluggish in a late

afternoon class, start class with an active game; or if they are overly energetic in a morning class, start with relaxation exercises.

Movement Manages Emotions

Movement is an effective means of shifting the function of the brain from survival mode to thinking and higher-order processes (Dennison and Dennison 1986, 1988; Promislow 1999; Hannaford 1995). Because the brain is wired for survival, it attends to stimuli with high emotional (pain or joy) content first. If the information is not interpreted as threatening, the frontal lobes are free to plan a response or action (Hannaford 1995; Jensen 1998a, b; Wolfe 2001). If the information is considered threatening, however, the flight-or-fight response kicks in, effectively closing down the higher-order thought processes as blood and glucose are redirected from the front brain, or cerebral cortex, to the hindbrain, or brain stem. This response does not allow the brain to make choices or consider new ideas (Hannaford 1995; Jensen 1998a, b; Promislow 1999; Wolfe 2001).

Movement also serves to relieve stress. If children live in a continual state of stress, the forebrain will not receive adequate circulation to func-

Getting your students moving is a great way to help them handle their emotions.

tion efficiently, because the survival center in the rear of the brain is on constant alert (Jensen 1998a, b; Promislow 1999; Wolfe 2001). Jensen (1998a, b) believes that high stress levels over time can reduce the ability of the brain to find means, form memories, understand, and develop higher-order thinking skills.

As physical educators, we have a powerful tool for learning because our classes elicit positive emotional effects in children. If learning takes place in a positive emotional context, students will remember what they learned because the release of epinephrine activates and stimulates the brain. In addition, because the brain learns holistically, students will remember the positive emotional aspects of a memory along with what they have learned when they access it in the future (Promislow 1999). Conversely, when negative emotion (shame, fear) is tied to learning, the memory recalled and assembled (in the future) of that experience will include the negative emotion (heightened stress), which can affect learning.

1. **Take into account the emotional component of children's past learning.** Take a show-of-hands poll to assess students' apprehension or excitement about class activities. Discuss positive aspects and relate those to students' lives. Address unpleasant experiences by relating personal experiences, disguising the disliked activity in a novel game, pairing it with a favored activity, or using tasks that allow success for students with a variety of skill levels.

2. **Give plenty of positive individual feedback.** Jensen (1998b) recommends that each child receive feedback every 30 minutes. Use a variety of modes (writing, movement, singing). Use scraps of paper to write notes to students. Allow peers to give feedback.

3. **Create appropriate levels of conflict or heightened emotion to focus and activate the brain.** Use debates and directed discussions about issues appropriate for school. Use competition, cooperative challenges, and personal bests. Leave some room for student interpretation, questioning, or opportunities to make choices, take risks, and be in charge.

4. **Provide opportunities for celebration within the class structure or unit.** Identify a student of the day, group of the week, or outstanding final performance. Have students use self-congratulations (e.g., pat themselves on the back) and encourage peer recognition. Implement award ceremonies and presentations of outstanding work. Recognize achievements in a public forum (Jensen 1998a).

5. **Create an event that can tie positive emotion to content.** Leave time for a class end-of-the-unit show, problem-solving (or other

thinking skill) tournament, health fair, or day for students to show off their best skills. Have older students present what they have learned to younger students. Include speakers, field trips, participation in a countywide contest, service learning opportunities, or other means of linking class content with the outside community.

6. **Teach children to recognize and deal with stress.** Stop to identify emotion as it occurs in class activities. Use high- and low-stress or high- and low-emotion activities to allow students to compare and contrast. Teach a process (relaxation exercises) and have a place (e.g., ice box or cool-down box, or think spot) for students to use when needed.

7. **Use class events to teach about appropriate responses to emotion.** Identify and model appropriate responses to stress when an incident occurs. Allow time for guided discussion. Use examples of current situations in the school or community. Have students role-play situations in groups and then report to the class.

8. **Allow students many opportunities to practice appropriate responses to stress.** Develop or adapt games to include relaxation exercise or reciting of class rules and procedures to get back into the game. Use exercise to reduce stress levels of individual students or the whole class. Have students review and act out stress-reduction and conflict resolution procedures often. For example, at the end of class, have a small number of students act out in soap opera form a situation that occurred (or make one up!) that caused some stress to the class. Allow students to exaggerate the situation in an appropriate way. Stop the acting (have actors freeze) at any time to ask, "What do you think will happen next?" or "Could this have been handled a different way?" Let the group finish. Discuss other endings or have other groups come up with and present another ending at the next class. End with an exercise to reduce stress (e.g., deep breathing).

Movement Demonstrates Learning

Development of specialized motor skills integrates knowledge and thinking with coordinated muscle movement. Information about spatial relationships, team dynamics, individual strategies, and achievement of goals is processed along with the motor plan. Skilled sport and dance movements allow people to communicate their knowledge to the outside world. Hannaford (1995) proposes that this ability to express oneself physically integrates knowledge and facilitates thought.

Brain-Compatible Movement Exercises

In general, brain-compatible movement exercises are designed to improve communication within the brain to support excellence in higher-order thinking skills and the ability to act; to reduce tension and thus stimulate use of the whole brain and promote the flow of electromagnetic energy within the body; to help the brain shift from thinking with the dominant (or preferred) hemisphere to allow both halves of the brain to work together; to assist blood flow, direct energy flow, and release muscle tension; and to activate and focus the brain to assist with concentration (Dennison and Dennison 1986, 1988; Hannaford 1995; Jensen 1998b; Promislow 1999).

Although a portion of the exercises discussed here will seem novel to physical educators, others will be familiar. The exercises and activities listed have been developed along the lines of the work of brain-friendly researchers and educators (e.g., Dennison and Dennison 1986, 1988).

Contralateral and Crossing-the-Midline Exercises

Hannaford (1995) suggests that simple whole-body integrative movements help children prepare to learn. *Contralateral movements* are those in which limbs on opposite sides of the body move at the same time to stimulate both hemispheres of the brain to work at the same time. The eyes also move in various paths as the limbs move (Dennison and Dennison 1986, 1988). Total-body movements that cause the limbs to cross the midline of the body to the opposite side can also force the hemispheres to work together. See figure 1.2 for sample contralateral and crossing-the-midline exercises.

Hydrate That Brain!

Water is necessary as a medium for transport of nutrients, oxygen, and waste products of cell metabolism. Adequate hydration improves concentration and coordination to aid in the development of academic skill. Most people do not drink enough water to support optimal brain function (Hannaford 1995). Promislow (1999) suggests 10 ounces of water for every 30 pounds (295 milliliters for every 13.6 kilograms) of body weight per day. To increase water intake, allow frequent drink breaks during the day, allow drinks before and after physical education class, encourage children to drink water instead of sweetened drinks, and teach the importance of water as a nutrient.

Contralateral and Crossing-the-Midline Exercises

Large Locomotor Skills

Have students exaggerate a skill by slowing it down and extending their leg and arm movements. The eyes should follow the limbs or focus on objects in the environment while the students move safely. Students should vary the speed at which they do the activity.

X Moves

Students start with the body in an X formation. They move the opposite arm and leg toward each other in different ways. For example, they can touch the hand to the toe, the knee to the elbow, or the wrist to the opposite hip. The eyes follow the movement of a limb. Have students try the exercises while sitting or lying on the ground.

X-tra Head, Shoulders, Knees, and Toes

Rather than perform the traditional movements to the song "Head, Shoulders, Knees and Toes," students start with the same sides touching (both hands to head) but then cross the arms to touch opposite sides. They can try it by alternating crossed and uncrossed arms.

Strings and Links

Have students imagine that their arms are connected by strings so that as they move, the other side must move in the same manner. They can try it with the legs and with the arms and legs together. They should try to link their eyes with movement of a limb.

X Routines

Have students develop a combination of contralateral moves. Add music and dance!

X Tag

Have students play a tag game, but to be safe they must perform a contralateral movement. To get back into the game, they must perform a series of contralateral movements.

Figure 1.2   Sample contralateral and crossing-the-midline exercises.

Exercises to Stimulate the Vestibular System

The vestibular system located near the ear provides information about the position of the head in space to assist with posture and balance. Stimulating the inner ear with spinning and turning or changes of posi-

Exercises to Stimulate the Vestibular System

Rhythms and Rocks

Students do rocking movements on various parts of the body, performing them to various tempos of music.

Egger

Students tuck the knees to the chest and rock the shoulders to the hips, from side to side or on the diagonal from the shoulder to the opposite hip.

Tummy Rocker

While lying on their bellies, students arch their backs enough to rock gently.

Strider

While standing in a side stride position, students rock from side to side or back to front in a front lunge position.

Partner Rocker

Partner A sits with knees flexed and feet together. Partner B sits on the feet of the partner A and tucks his or her feet under the seat of the partner A. With arms extended, partners hold each other's shoulders while they rock.

Spins and Turns

Students try rotary movements, done under control for safety, on various parts of the body at various speeds and levels.

Figure 1.3   Sample exercises to stimulate the vestibular system.

tion alerts the brain to sensory stimuli (Hannaford 1995). These types of activities help children set up the neural pathways necessary for effective communication within the brain to support balance and posture needed for learning (see figure 1.3).

Stretching Exercises

Brain-based programs identify an additional benefit of stretching, that of helping the brain get ready for learning and thinking. By reducing muscle tension or fatigue in specialized areas of the body, stretching can help the brain move from survival mode to integrated, whole-use mode (Dennison and Dennison 1986, 1988; Hannaford 1995). Emphasize returning the muscle to its natural length or condition by not overstretching the muscle and by performing stretching exercises slowly.

In concert with stretching, deep breathing increases oxygen to the body, relaxes the muscles, and assists the brain in receiving and processing information (Hannaford 1995).

Aerobic Exercise

Aerobic fitness benefits brain function by increasing blood flow to the brain and by elevating the mood through the release of endorphins. Exercise strengthens the cerebellum and corpus callosum (Jensen 1998a, b); allows the nerves to communicate better (Kinoshita 1997); and improves memory (Brink 1995), response time to a stimulus (Jensen 1998a, b), and cognitive function (e.g., Hannaford 1995; Michaud and Wild 1991; Martens 1982). Exercise may be one of the best ways to stimulate the brain and learning capacity (Brink 1995; Silverman 1993).

Gardner's Learning Frames in Physical Education

One important brain-based theory that has had an effect on traditional modes of instruction is Howard Gardner's theory of multiple intelligences (1993). This theory relates to the preferences that a child may develop for how he or she acquires information. Gardner has identified a core of capabilities that underlies a specific frame of intelligence. Each person has capabilities in each area identified as an intelligence, yet each person differs in the ability to use these capabilities. Each type of intelligence interacts with the others to allow the person to function in a variety of tasks (Armstrong 2000; Gardner 1993).

To be effective, physical educators must teach to all the intelligences. Refer to table 1.1 for assistance in developing lessons or units that address multiple frames of mind. For any content, activity, or game, select one to three different means to present. The work of Gardner and others in this area has caused many teachers to adopt active-learning strategies to assist children who use modes other than linguistic and logical–mathematical to find success in the classroom (Gardner 1993; Armstrong 2000).

Each activity in this book identifies which of the learning styles it addresses.

Table 1.1 Gardner's Multiple Intelligences

Type of intelligence	Think	Core components or abilities	Instructional tips
Linguistic (L)	In words	Able to use words (oral or written) well	Present orally and in writing. Refer to children's literature, linguistic structure, and vocabulary. Use task cards or written instructions. Allow the student to answer orally or in writing. Let the student be the commentator, peer leader, or announcer. Let the student use or make an audio tape recording. Allow time for students to share orally or in writing with peers. Ask the student to "talk through" a task or concept while others demonstrate. Permit choral answers.
Logical–mathematical (LM)	By reasoning	Uses numbers well

Identifies and develops patterns and relationships

Can form and understand abstractions | Use numbers in instruction. Be logical in presentations. Give reasons for content. Collect numerical data. Allow the student to compose, identify patterns, classify, and categorize. Incorporate problem solving. Encourage the student to practice critical thinking. Encourage the student to produce movement in a logical framework. Ask for reasons for movement responses. Use experiments to support concepts. |
| Spatial (S) | In images and pictures | Perceives and uses space accurately | Allow use of space to represent ideas. Use charts, diagrams, video, and visual puzzles. Include imaginative activities. Encourage use of mind maps. Include visual awareness activities. Have the student identify visual patterns. Give opportunities to draw and graph. Have the student see it, draw or diagram it, or color it. Give opportunities to design and manipulate space. |

(continued)

Table 1.1 *continued*

Type of intelligence	Think	Core components or abilities	Instructional tips
Bodily–kinesthetic (K)	As they experience movement	Controls body movements Handles objects skillfully Uses body for expression	Include hands-on thinking. Use movement to illustrate concepts. Use movement examples in explanations. Use kinesthetic imagery. Incorporate use of manipulatives. Have the student use the body to communicate ideas. Allow practice in fine and gross motor activities. Have students act out concepts or ideas singly or in groups.
Musical (M)	Via rhythms and melodies	Produces and appreciates rhythm, pitch, and timbre Understands forms of musical expression	Use music or concepts in presentations. Play music in the background. Include group singing. Link concepts with melodies. Have the student develop songs or melodies to movement. Allow the student to identify or apply musical structure. Have the student use movement to music.
Interpersonal (IE)	By interacting with others	Discriminates between own preferences and those of another	Allow team- or cooperative work. Give the opportunity to teach. Encourage group process. Allow the student to function as a group mediator or leader. Encourage peer or group sharing.
Intrapersonal (IA)	In relation to one's self	Is in tune with own feelings, strengths, and weaknesses	Give opportunities for individual activities. Allow space and time for private practice. Individualize instruction. Use journal writing. Encourage goal setting. Give options for task completion. Allow time for self-reflection. Have the student connect content to personal life.

Type of intelligence	Think	Core components or abilities	Instructional tips
Naturalistic (N)	Through nature forms	Distinguishes between species Sees relationships	Use categorizations and concepts from nature. Use nature themes in movement settings. Relate skills and concepts to the natural world. Act out processes common in nature.

Columns 1 and 2 adapted from T. Armstrong, 2000, *Multiple intelligences in the classroom,* 2nd ed. (Alexandria, VA: Association for Supervision and Curriculum Development), 22. Adapted by permission. The Association for Supervision and Curriculum Development is a worldwide community of educators advocating sound policies and sharing best practices to achieve the success of each learner. To learn more, visit ASCD at www.ascd.org. Columns 3 and 4 adapted from Gardner 1993.

Types of Thinking

To *think* is to be consciously aware of cognitive information (thoughts called up from long-term memory) and then manipulate this information in a variety of ways (in various parts of the brain) to meet a particular goal (e.g., find an answer, find meaning, solve a problem) (Beyer 1987; Ruggiero 1985). In physical education, movement can be not only the product of a thinking process but also the means by which the student acquires skill in thinking (Hannaford 1995).

Thinking is made up of subsets of discrete skills that are organized in a hierarchy. Discrete skills linked with a knowledge base can be combined in various ways to yield complex thinking operations or processes (Beyer 1987; Ennis 1986; Swartz and Perkins 1990). These processes are often organized into categories that are set into a structure, or *taxonomy.* Possibly the most well known model of thinking for educators is Bloom's taxonomy (see table 1.2). Bloom (1956) identified levels of thinking operations to encourage educators to develop educational objectives. Bloom desired to move teachers beyond rote memorization, comprehension, and application to address a fuller range of cognitive abilities. Many educators believe that the top three levels in Bloom's hierarchy—analysis, synthesis, and evaluation—are the highest order of thinking skills.

Thinking skills can be categorized not only to assist in the writing of educational objectives but also according to the specific goal or intended outcome of the thinking task (Swartz and Perkins 1989). As physical educators, we need to include not only the National Association for Sport and Physical Education (2004) standards in physical education but also dispositions, attributes, or habits to support the use of movement

Table 1.2   Bloom's Taxonomy of Educational Objectives

Objective	Description
Knowledge	Recalls facts, concepts, and terms. Answers.
Comprehension	Understands. Can compare, organize, describe, translate, state the main idea, and interpret.
Application	Applies facts and knowledge in new ways. Can solve problems.
Analysis	Breaks information into parts. Can make inferences. Finds evidence and discovers causes and motives. Can generalize.
Synthesis	Can put together information in new ways and determine alternative solutions.
Evaluation	Can make judgments based on criteria, quality, and information. Can present and defend opinions.

and thinking skills (Ennis 1986; Paul 1992). All these components of thinking, discrete skills, processes, and dispositions linked with rules and strategies for use, intertwine to promote effective thinking (Beyer 1987) and movement production. Four major categories of thinking are discussed here: *acquiring knowledge, creative thinking, critical thinking,* and *metacognition.* For each category, specific thinking skills are identified. These skills are the basis for a thinking curriculum. Depending on your curricular goals, you can select one or more of the skills to emphasize in your teaching. For your convenience, each of this book's activities lists the thinking skills used and reinforced in the activity.

Acquiring Knowledge

In movement settings, this type of thinking—acquiring knowledge—is necessary to store and then organize and recall memories (information), solve movement challenges, learn the names of skills, understand movement concepts, learn principles of fitness, learn the steps to a dance, and so on. Positive dispositions for acquiring knowledge are curiosity, perseverance, and willingness to try to make sense out of what is presented. Specific thinking skills related to acquiring knowledge include the following (Beyer 1987, Bloom 1956, Quellmalz 1986, Sternberg 1983, Swartz and Perkins 1990).

- **Recalling (remembering).** Remember or locate memories (e.g., "Who can remember a term we learned today?").

- **Relating (telling).** Connect information to tell or show (e.g., "Tell me what you remember" or "Show me a hop").

- **Identification (naming).** Remember and name (e.g., "What do we call this move?" or "The principle we are using is called?").

- **Clarification (explaining).** Describe; use related memories to help with understanding (e.g., "Refine your movement" or "Explain to your peer which exercise is aerobic and which is muscle endurance").

- **Classification.** Arrange, organize, or sort into categories (e.g., "Put all the fast moves together" or "Decide which exercises are appropriate to use for warming up").

- **Comparison and contrast.** Identify similarities and differences (e.g., "How is this move different or the same?" or "Show me a move that is very different").

- **Illustrating.** Come up with examples and similar instances (e.g., "Show me a new or different way this concept could be shown" or "Where have you used this concept in your life at home?").

- **Ordering (ranking).** Sort information or arrange it in a sequence (e.g., "Present your moves from large to small" or "Be sure your dance has a beginning, middle, and end").

- **Recognizing patterns.** Identify and name a design or arrangement (e.g., "What does this move remind you of?" or "Can anyone identify a pattern in what we are doing?").

- **Generalizing.** Develop an overview or simplification of a set of information (e.g., "What do we call all of these types of movement?" or "All of the games we have played this week have what in common?").

- **Summarizing.** Concisely state or review the main points in a set of information (e.g., "In a few words, tell me what happened" or "Give me one move that is representative of what we did in class today").

- **Analysis.** Break information down and examine the parts, then assemble the parts into a whole (e.g., "What moves are part of a layup?").

- **Application.** Use information in different ways, or relate information in new ways to other subjects (e.g., "Use this move in a game situation" or "How could you be more active at home?").

Creative Thinking

In physical education classes, creativity is generating new ideas and perspectives. It is a part of every movement used in a new way or as part of a novel combination of movements. Developing a dance from the perspective of a Native American, producing a novel shot on goal in a soccer game, or assembling a unique combination of a twisting movement with two body parts are examples of movement that use creative thinking. Viewing a situation from a different perspective, taking risks, being adventurous, and being willing to try something new are dispositions helpful for creative thinking (Swartz and Perkins 1990). Specific thinking skills related to creative thinking include the following (Ennis 1986, Ruggiero 1991, Swartz and Perkins 1990).

- **Variety (divergent reasoning).** From a common starting point, come up with a variety of movements (e.g., "How many different ways can you pass the ball?" or "Show me moves you have seen in the winter Olympics").
- **Novelty (originality).** Create a new move; produce movement in a fresh, different manner or use known movement in a new way (e.g., "Show me a new way to shoot the ball" or "Can you develop a new way to skip?").
- **Elaboration.** Add to your move; take an idea or movement and add learned information to it (e.g., "Now take the game you have developed and add a new rule for scoring" or "Now add two changes of level").
- **Composition.** Arrange your moves; position ideas or movements together in an innovative manner or develop a new idea or move from already learned ones (e.g., "Put these individual gymnastic movements together in a new way" or "How would you use the strategies we learned in tag games in a flag football game?").
- **Synthesis.** Blend your moves; combine or apply ideas or movements into a new form or original concept (e.g., "Blur the edges of your movements to make it took like one continuous move" or "Make up a new game").

Critical Thinking

We use critical thinking to answer the question "Why?" In essence, critical thinking raises the bar on ordinary thinking when making a judgment or decision. A critical thinker becomes her or his own evaluator and critic as she or he strives to get it right (Ennis 2000a) to produce a better product or outcome (Swartz and Perkins 1990). To be an effective critical thinker, the person must be willing to suspend all personal beliefs and values to determine an impartial and reason-based justification for the thought product, process, or act. In physical education, students use critical thinking when they provide reasons for using a particular play in a game, explain a strategy from the perspective of a defender, or determine why a cooperative group failed to meet criteria for a successful movement product. Specific thinking skills related to critical thinking include the following (Beyer 1987, Buschner 1990, Norris and Ennis 1989).

- **Objective observation.** Examine information from an unbiased perspective (e.g., "Try to leave your personal likes and dislikes out of your observation and repeat the movement exactly as I performed it").

- **Focus.** Direct attention as requested (e.g., "Watch the entire dance pattern" or "Remember, we are trying to show stillness through our movements").

- **Discernment.** Recognize pertinent and factual information as distinct from irrelevant or incorrect information (e.g., "What do you need to know to complete this project?" or "How do you know that this is the correct way to perform this drill? Who told you? How do you know it is correct?").

- **Hypothesis.** Make educated guesses based on facts (e.g., "Ask a question that will help you to understand" or "What do you think will happen next? Why?").

- **Causal reasoning.** See connections between cause and effect (e.g., "If the ball is here, then where should the defense set up?")

- **Conditional reasoning.** Make decisions based on circumstances that have occurred or will occur (e.g., "For us to produce this movement pattern, what has to occur?" or "If we are to be healthy adults, what do we need to do now?").

- **Tolerance of ambiguity.** Think or perform in situations that lack clarity or have no absolutely right or wrong answer (e.g., "From what we know, let's try to play the game" or "Continue to work on your dance—you will figure out the timing!").

- **Clarity.** Ask pertinent questions in search of missing information; ask "why?" (e.g., "Who has a question they need answered?").

- **View a situation from a variety of perspectives** (e.g., "How would you do this move if you were a hip-hop dancer?" or "Look at this fitness program as if you were the one to use it").

- **Identifying personal biases.** Understand and articulate desires, likes, dislikes, and preferences (e.g., "Why did you pick that play to run?" or "Why do you like the first movement activities more than the second one?")

- **Justification.** Give reasons for decisions based on logic and facts (e.g., "Can you explain why you added that new move to your routine?" or "Tell me why you decided to include flexibility exercises in your program").
- **Reflection.** Analyze actions and seek to improve or retain (e.g., "Think back over the semester: what one thing did you learn that you will use in your free time?" or "Why are you unhappy with your performance?").
- **Evaluation.** Assign worth or value to a judgment or decision (e.g., "How did your team perform?").

Metacognition

Metacognition is, simply put, thinking about thinking. How many times have students in a game situation said, "I should have . . ."? The thinking involved with the decision in this case would be examined to determine how to make a better decision the next time. In individual skill work, asking a student how he or she came up with such a creative movement asks the student to identify the thought process that he or she used. Students use metacognition when they reflect on the thought process used to refine a dance routine or explain how their group arrived at the decision to include a particular move. Specific thinking skills related to critical thinking include the following (Swartz and Perkins 1990).

- **Identify the thinking skill being used.** "What thinking skill are we using here?"
- **Decide which thinking skill should be used.** "What thinking process will we need to use to complete this problem?"
- **Pay attention to the thinking process.** "What are the steps we need to follow to develop this exercise sequence?"
- **Reflect on one's own thinking process in relation to a specific outcome.** "How are you thinking? What are you thinking? How did the thinking process you used work in designing this dance?"

Specialized Thinking Processes

Clusters of discrete thinking skills, or lower-level thinking processes, can be combined to address a specific complex problem. These processes include more steps to complete and involve integration with a larger knowledge base. Types of specialized thinking used in physical education are *reflection, problem solving, decision making, goal setting,* and *planning.* Each type can stand alone as a process or be used in varying combination with others (Swartz and Perkins 1990).

Reflection

Reflection is a thinking process in which the person carefully examines an act, event, response, or process (usually what has happened in the past but also to plan for the future) to assess or gain understanding of it. Thinking about what went wrong in a game, thinking about how one felt when performance was not up to par, or thinking about how to use in the future what was learned that day are examples of reflective thinking. The student can then act to adjust, change, or determine the next course of action. Reflection should result in affirmation or a call to change (Norris and Ennis 1989).

To encourage reflection, you must allow time for students to think more deeply than they can with simple recollection, or recall. By establishing criteria, you allow students to assess a situation according to the stated criteria. In addition, students need to recognize the role of their personal values and beliefs in guiding their thoughtful consideration, be willing to examine their actions, and want to improve. Basic thinking skills that contribute to reflection include analysis, comparison and contrast, causal reasoning, and conditional reasoning (Nickerson 1987, Norris and Ennis 1989, Swartz and Perkins 1990). All four categories of thinking can be called on when reflection is used.

It's important to allow your students plenty of time for reflection.

In a physical education setting, reflection could be shown in a discussion like this following a creative movement sequence: "All groups have developed a creative movement sequence that is interesting and fun to watch, but now you need to switch your emphasis to the criteria for your performance. Let's take some quiet time right now to think about your performance in your own head carefully and critically. How can *you* make it better? Now discuss your suggestions with your group; each member in your group must contribute one idea."

Problem Solving

Problem solving involves the identification and analysis of a dilemma or predicament. After clearly defining the problem, the person reflects on causes and reasons for its development to assist in generating a number of reasonable and creative solutions. The person critically examines each solution for its positive and negative aspects to pare down the list to a few best alternatives. These alternatives are implemented and then assessed for worthiness in addressing the problem. The person selects the best or most feasible solution, or he or she may scrap them all and begin the process again (Bransford, Sherwood, and Sturdevant 1986). Problem-solving activities allow students in physical education to be directly engaged in learning and benefit from their successes and failures (Ocansey 1994).

To be a good problem solver a student must recognize that a problem exists, explore a variety of solutions, and follow a step-by-step process to solve the problem. The basic thinking skills that support problem solving include identification, analysis, variety, causal reasoning, relating parts and whole, novelty, ordering, identifying personal biases, and hypothesis (Swartz and Perkins 1990). Components from all categories of thinking are helpful in learning to solve problems.

An example of problem solving in a movement setting might be if you were to ask students, "Decide how you will travel across the space with your feet making as little sound as possible. Try out three different ways to move with 'quiet' feet. In a few minutes I will ask you to show me your best solution."

Decision Making

Decision making is a hybrid form of problem solving. It differs from problem solving in that the person must make one choice in response to the evaluation of a variety of possible options when no one clear or completely correct option is available. The person evaluates all the potential alternatives at the same time and then ranks them without having the opportunity to test the best alternatives. By narrowing the ranks with reflection, additional analysis, and further evaluation, the person determines one best "guess" (Bransford, Sherwood, and Sturdevant 1986;

Quellmalz 1986). This process involves a measure of risk because the response, although well intended, may not be the best one or may not be suited to a changing situation in a dynamic movement setting (e.g., when the defense switches to zone or the music is a faster tempo than usual).

To make good decisions, an individual must recognize that a decision is needed and want to find the most reasonable solution while recognizing his or her own personal biases or preferences. Thinking skills which contribute to decision making include discernment, objective observation, causal reasoning, variety, novelty, elaboration, hypothesis, ordering, justification, analysis, and comparison and contrast (Swartz and Perkins 1990).

You can guide your students in making decisions by using four simple "what" questions:

- What do we need to do?
- What are our options? (Any suggestions?)
- What will work best?
- What is our decision?

Goal Setting

Goal setting includes identifying a clear purpose, aim, outcome, or target after identifying and assembling pertinent information to assist in its formation. Goal determination essentially is a problem-solving or decision-making process that reflects the needs and values of the person or group involved. The person or group must develop the goal after critically examining available evidence, assessing the potential to attain the goal, and considering any problems or factors that could affect achievement of the goal. Thoughtful consideration of personal interests and needs must be part of the process, and established goals must be of value to the person or people involved. The views of the individual must to varying degrees be integrated or rejected while the viewpoints of others are carefully considered. Students will need assistance in defining goals and including evaluative criteria that they can use later to monitor progress, assess goal attainment, and evaluate the goal-setting process. Basic skills that support goal setting include analysis, generalizing, synthesis, justification, and conditional reasoning.

An example of how goal setting could work in the physical education class is the use of fitness test results to improve personal fitness: "After receiving the data from the fitness battery we completed, identify one area of fitness you feel you could improve. Tell me in your log why you would like to improve this area, what the change would be, and one example of how you could begin to work toward your goal."

Planning

Planning is the upfront work necessary for producing a thought, generating a movement response, or achieving a goal. Planning includes the development of a step-by-step schema, method, or framework with the intent of achieving a goal or purpose (e.g., to implement a solution, achieve a high grade, or decide how to improve scoring opportunities). Knowledge of previous plans and creativity in adapting or formulating new plans are essential. Planning can range from a process composed of a few steps to a complex list of many detailed tasks. To develop planning skills, students need a clear idea of the product, the criteria, an appropriate model to follow, and time to develop the plan. Basic skills that are helpful in planning include discernment, relating parts and whole, causal reasoning, variety, composition, conditional reasoning, and analysis. One example of planning in physical education would be to tell students, "Your group has three class periods until your final dance is due. I will give you 20 minutes of each class to prepare. Sit down with your group and lay out a plan for how you will use the time to complete your project. Hand it in to me before you leave."

Conclusion

Although thinking is clearly an important part of movement activities and games, teaching thinking has not been an important part of physical education curriculum in the past. But using the physical education class to build skills that support knowledge, develop individual and group strategies, and create new movement products can help students become better movers and thinkers. Intentionally assisting students to use thinking skills and processes effectively within the physical education curriculum further supports the value of physical education in students' learning experience.

CHAPTER 2

Teaching Thinking Through Physical Activity

At this point, the thought of integrating a thinking emphasis in physical education may seem overwhelming. You begin, of course, by making a decision to try and then reflecting on what the goal or product of the thinking curriculum will be. Schwager and Labate (1993) note that many teachers already incorporate critical-thinking skills without realizing that they are doing so. This section will introduce suggestions to begin moving toward teaching thinking in physical education and then will offer a plan on how to design an individualized thinking curriculum. In addition, the chapter includes a section on assessing the teaching of thinking in your physical education curriculum.

Moving Toward a Thinking Curriculum

You might feel as if you need to create an intricate new curriculum to begin teaching thinking skills, incorporating a vast array of skills within your yearly teaching plan. But take a deep breath and relax! You can start by making a few simple changes to your existing curriculum. The best approach is to start small, selecting just a few skills to focus on in your curriculum. Beyer (1987) proposes that teachers select two to four thinking skills or processes to teach within a subject area within an academic year. Sherman (1999) suggests that teachers devote at least 20 weeks of instruction to a specific thinking process to allow time for adequate practice for students and to allow students to benefit from their learning. Starting small increases the chances of success, both by making the task manageable for you and by allowing students plenty of time to learn and practice their new skills.

Explicit or Embedded Teaching of Thinking?

Before determining how to fit thinking within physical education, you must decide what the driving force will be. Will the physical education curriculum yield opportunities to teach identified thinking content, or will you impose an identified thinking model on the physical education curriculum?

Developing the content for teaching thinking could be an *explicit* approach. You might teach a thinking skill and then manipulate the content area of the subject to address the thinking skill. You define a single process from the model, give examples, and model the process in the movement setting. Students practice and then use the skills in a variety of movement and classroom applications (Beyer 1987). This approach is meant to support thinking taught in other academic areas and eventually to transfer it into use in situations outside school.

In an *embedded,* or *infused,* style of teaching, you identify the thinking content as it should or will occur within the sport or movement curriculum and then emphasize it as it presents itself. With an embedded approach to content development, the learning of thinking is more meaningful to the student. Once you develop the content or model, you must present the thinking process within the normal context of a physical education lesson (Blitzer 1995). When a situation occurs, or when a planned experience or an opportunity presents itself, you teach or review the thinking skill. Instructors using this style need to examine and then develop activities within the unit where the thinking skills will be needed and plan to teach them. The best method may be a combination of the two—the explicit approach to introduce the concept and the embedded style to refine and clarify the concept.

Adopt a Student-Centered Teaching Style

One approach that can move your curriculum toward supporting thinking is to use a student-centered style of teaching in which students take on more of the responsibility for learning by producing movement responses using their own interpretations and understanding of the task (Werner 1995). Some ideas about how to increase the thinking that already is happening in your physical education class include the following:

- Encourage students to discover answers, instead of giving them the answers.
- Ask many questions. Ask hard questions! Answer a question with a question. Or ask other students for help.
- Use cooperative learning or add group work to lessons.
- Talk through your thinking aloud as you solve problems (or use other thinking processes).
- Allow time for thinking. Ponder and wait to answer. Make students think before answering.
- Give positive feedback on "good" thinking!
- Set up activities in which students must figure out what to do (leave out a key instruction, have different equipment available than what the instruction calls for, give a goal for a task and have students come up with the activity).
- Let students fix their own problems.
- Model good thinking.
- Use brain-compatible strategies to help with learning.

Select Curricular Approaches That Support Thinking

Another place to start is to supplement your curriculum with models that inherently offer the opportunity to emphasize thinking skills. Two models that support elements of thinking are *movement education* and *adventure education and initiatives.* Both models integrate problem solving and decision making with movement (Placek and Sullivan 1997). A third curricular emphasis, *cooperative learning,* is an excellent means to start to integrate thinking skills and dispositions (McBride 1999).

Consider examining what other researchers and teachers have already attempted in physical education settings and then adopt it or adjust it as needed. A good start would be the special edition of the *Journal of Physical Education, Recreation and Dance* on critical thinking and physical education edited by McBride in 1995. Others have introduced their own approaches (Ennis 1991; McBride 1992; McBride and Bonnette 1995; Schwager and Labate 1993; Sherman 1999; Tishman and Perkins 1995) or have reported on real-life applications within physical education settings (Choo and Jewel 2001; Gerney 1993; Ocansey 1994; Rovengno et al. 1995; Savoy 1971; Stillman 1989; West 1989; Woods and Bok 1995).

Consider Students' Needs and Abilities

To determine the types of thinking skills to emphasize, you must consider the cognitive development or ability of the students. One important developmental factor to consider is that to use the higher-order thinking centers of the brain, the movement with which thinking is integrated must be learned well enough to be relegated to the cerebellum for production. If the skill is not well laid down in neural pathways, the cerebral cortex must organize the movement and will not be available to apply the thinking skill. In physical education, the cognitive operations may need to take a back seat until students learn the motor skills sufficiently. For example, asking students to problem solve how to move quickly through an obstacle course while dribbling a ball will be difficult unless they can perform the skill of dribbling without having to think about it (thus allowing them to focus on the obstacle course).

Besides using your experiential knowledge of your students' needs, you should examine state curricula and the results of state testing to identify which thinking skills to teach. Discussions with classroom teachers in other academic areas can be extremely helpful.

Choose Skills to Teach

The thinking skills and processes emphasized in academic settings have been influenced by state requirements, testing, and the kinds of thinking needed for success in disciplines other than physical education (McBride and Bonnette 1995). Suggestions to help identify the specific content of a thinking curriculum are listed here. Select a few components to emphasize in the physical education curriculum.

- Determine what thinking model is emphasized in the school.
- Examine curricular documents for grade levels to determine what thinking operations teachers are using in other classes.
- Talk to classroom teachers to find out what they are emphasizing in instruction and whether they can identify any weaknesses or strengths in thinking that physical education content could address.
- Study the information presented in this book and assemble a list of potential thinking components, basic and specialized, to use with physical education content.
- Examine the National Association for Sport and Physical Education standards (2004) to identify what thinking skills are necessary to develop a "physically educated person" (see table 2.1).
- Examine specific physical education content areas and emphasize one or two thinking skills necessary for success in that area (e.g., in basketball, recognition and decision making).
- Consult with researchers or theorists in the field of thinking. According to Beyer (1987), skills that underlie all others are *conceptualizing, identification of attributes,* and *classification.* Bloom's taxonomy is another potential choice. Other models may also be useful (e.g., Costa, Ennis, Beyer, Sternberg).

Designing a Thinking Curriculum Model

If none of the approaches presented earlier in this chapter appear to be the right match for a particular teaching situation or if a ready-made model is not appropriate, the next best approach is to design a specific curriculum model to meet the needs of the school, physical education program, and students. A thinking model should show a hierarchy of content from lower-level to higher-order thinking, from simple to complex processes, and should show how the curriculum will be taught across time (e.g., across five grades in elementary school).

Table 2.1   Thinking Skills Taught to Address NASPE Standard 1

Standard 1: Demonstrates competency in motor skills and movement patterns needed to perform a variety of physical activities

Thinking category	Thinking skills identified within the standard
Acquiring knowledge	Know and perform (recall, identify, clarify)
	Refine (identify parts and wholes, compare and contrast, analyze)
	Apply and generalize
Creative thinking	Versatility in use (divergent reasoning, elaboration)
	Combine (composition, synthesis)
	Variety
Critical thinking	Decision making (observe objectively, consider a variety of views or approaches, identify assumptions and biases, justify decisions)

After determining the specific thinking content, you should examine it for any underlying lower-order skills that you may need to address or assess before teaching the identified higher-order skill. For example, before introducing problem solving, depending on the process taught, you may need to address skills such as compare and contrast, analysis, and elements of critical thinking and reflection.

For a more comprehensive approach, after you have tentatively identified the goals or the skills and processes that you might teach, use the following steps to help you develop a teaching model.

1. **Develop a goal or goals for the thinking curriculum and a rationale to guide the formation of the model.** A well-conceived rationale will help clarify the skills and order of importance to inform parents and administrators what the physical education program is attempting to accomplish.

2. **Select the skills and processes that you will teach.** When accomplished, this content will address and accomplish the goal for the curriculum. Selection of skills could evolve as already discussed in this chapter, or you could choose processes from another model. Remember to select a small number, two to four per year.

3. **Group skills or processes into categories or levels.** After deciding on the content, you should group skills or processes. The skills that you group together should have some relationship to each other, and you should place each component in only one category. Do not include too much. Better to teach a few things well than to be too broad.

4. **Group categories into a framework or structure.** You could arrange the groupings from less to more complex, cluster them around a common goal or concept, or perhaps divide them into separate categories in order of what needs to be accomplished first, second, and so on. Develop a label for each category.

5. **Adjust the terminology of the model to fit the learning level of the students.** The content must be understandable to the students involved. The terms can be catchy or creative, but they should be consistent with terminology already taught in the school to assist with transfer from the gymnasium back to the classroom.

6. **Let others review the model and give feedback.** At this point you will find it helpful to let others—peers, administrators, and even students—examine the model, offer suggestions, and express concerns. This process is especially helpful in making sure that the model communicates what you intended and addresses the goal or goals for the curriculum.

7. **Choose and implement the model.** After developing the model, you must break it down into components that you can introduce in lessons.

8. **Refine the model as needed.** The model will continue to need fine-tuning as you add physical education content. Adjust as needed to fit the needs of the students and school, meet the curricular goals, and be attainable in the time allotted.

Developing Thinking Lesson Plans

After you have chosen the model and the content development piece, the next step is to look at the physical education curriculum and develop the lessons in which you can specifically teach thinking skills. This process entails developing tasks or activities that address the thinking elements. Beyer (1987) suggests that a lesson should introduce the skill, allow for experimentation, and then invite students to think reflectively about their performance. A typical lesson taught by Rovengno et al. (1995) in a tag games unit included the practice of a basic skill or strategy followed by group work in which students designed and played games that incorporated the basic skills taught. Students then evaluated, modified, and played the revised games. The following steps and considerations describe the process of lesson development (Quellmalz 1986).

1. Define the content to be included in the lesson.

2. Develop learning objectives.

3. Identify any potential past learning (perhaps in the classroom), experiences, or movement activities that students may have

practiced or accomplished to help them identify patterns and related memories to link with the new information.

4. Identify where in the content of the lesson the targeted thinking skills are already included or could be addressed.

5. Develop examples, analogies, illustrations, diagrams, charts, movement tasks, and experiences to support learning.

6. Develop the teaching plan to incorporate movement and thinking tasks and allow opportunities to practice.

7. Prepare to model the process for students. Be sure to explain how learning the process will be helpful to students in their everyday lives.

8. Design practice opportunities for the students under simple conditions. Consider using cooperative learning groups.

9. Prepare to give plenty of individual feedback on the process.

10. Develop a task that assesses metacognition skills to assess students' learning and correct problems.

11. Plan for repeated practice.

12. At the end of the lesson discuss the use of the skill in varied contexts.

13. Plan to come back to the skill repeatedly in succeeding lessons for review and reinforcement.

Real-World Strategies

Besides identifying what an effective teacher already would use in any instructional setting, several authors and researchers have identified techniques to consider along with multiple intelligences and brain-compatible strategies when attempting to teach thinking and movement.

- **Teach for transfer.** You should show students the application of a thinking skill or process in a game situation and then show how they can use the same process in a variety of other situations. Learners need to consider the similarities between the thinking process as they use it in physical education class and as they use it in other academic areas. You should also ask where or when they are currently applying or could apply the skills in their personal or community lives (Swartz 1986).

- **Model the application.** You can help students learn to think by deliberately modeling the process in class (Freeland 1995). Take students step by step through the process, give examples, and talk

Model the types of thinking techniques you'd like your students to learn.

aloud through class-oriented and real-life examples. You also need to show that a problem has many potential answers and that even the best answer may not be entirely correct. As a model, you must be impartial, skillful, and willing to hold judgment until sufficient credible evidence is available (Nickerson 1986).

- **Use feedback.** Just as you would give specific positive feedback in motor skill learning, you should deliver feedback and show interest in students' learning of thinking skills. You should teach students how to recognize pertinent feedback for themselves after a task and how to use the feedback to improve skill performance. This act supports the development of reflective skills, analysis, error detection, and evaluation (Sherman 1999). Using peers to give feedback on thinking skills or motor performance is another method of informing students about their performance. The student assessor has the opportunity to use the skills of evaluation and analysis in an authentic situation. Asking students to give peer feedback serves a dual purpose. The receiver must use the brain to hear, interpret, and respond. The giver must assess, analyze, compare and contrast, and form a response (Jensen 1998b). Emphasize kindness as students critique each other's work (Rovengno et al. 1995).

- **Ask plenty of questions.** Simply asking questions after students' statements, decisions, or movement responses can cause them to use thinking skills and processes. Students' responses and reasons can give insight into the processes that they are using to develop answers. Ask questions that force students to reflect on their actions, and then dig deeper for specifics. Open-ended questions with no right answer may stimulate students to answer more creatively (Potts 1994). Using questions during debriefing sessions can focus students on the process and help them think about the thinking skills and processes (Kamla and Lindauer 2002).

- **Encourage students to ask questions.** Students who can ask questions have used thinking processes. You need not answer students' questions. You can return the question by asking, "What do you think about that?" or "What do you think is the answer?" This practice allows students to reveal the basis for the question and frame their thoughts about it. Asking other students for input allows more development of and exchange of ideas. This method also puts students in a position to begin to answer their own questions rather than always look to an adult for the answer (Johnson 1997). Questions from peers allow students more opportunity to explain or defend their ideas or comments. You will need to model appropriate questions and behaviors. Effective listening to peers is another skill that you may need to model and teach (Rovengno et al. 1995).

- **Allow time for discussion.** In physical education, the thrust should be movement and physical activity, yet discussion is also valuable. Discussion time gives students the opportunity to develop and express their thoughts, attitudes, and feelings. You are then privy to the processes in use, the attitudes being developed, and the depth of content knowledge. Discussions do not need to be time consuming. To allow for interpretation and creativity, use controversial but appropriate topics or ask questions with more than one possible answer. Draw on realistic situations. Ensure an atmosphere of acceptance for questions and responses posed by students. Identifying the question with the name of the asker can help students own their statements (Ennis 2000b). Rephrasing the question for clarity is a good practice to model because the rephrasing allows students to hear their thoughts.

- **Debrief after learning activities.** Debriefing helps students reflect on the thinking process and helps you assess group interaction. A debriefing session reviews and emphasizes key content; allows time for questions, clarifications, and concerns; and helps students cool down from the activity. The debriefing should end the session on a positive note.

- **Allow time for processing answers or responses.** Waiting for students to think could be the one technique that will have the greatest effect on success in answering questions (Johnson 1997) or completing thinking processes (Werner 1995). Sometimes teachers believe that time not filled with words or action is wasted. But the brain needs time to plow through the pertinent sensory and stored information to draw connections, patterns, and relationships. Wait time helps students understand that they are supposed to think deeply and that the quick answer is not necessarily the best response (Potts 1994). Although waiting in silence may be uncomfortable for students and teacher alike, Johnson (1997) suggests waiting three seconds in physical education classes before moving to encourage, repeat, or prompt. Encourage students to use processing time for planning, mental practice, or self-talk (metacognition) before they respond to a question or begin a task.

- **Encourage thinking from another perspective.** Ask students to respond to a movement task or question from the perspective of a peer, teacher, member of the opposite gender, member on another team, or a famous person. This approach forces students to move beyond their personal points of view and develop novel insights and responses not formerly possible. Teaching students to be considerate of others' thoughts, moves, and responses is a difficult but important task. Effective thinkers must consider how their decisions may affect others. You may need to teach students skills in communication and emotion management. One of the reasons for teaching thinking and reasoning is to help students learn alternative ways to deal with disagreement (Nickerson 1986).

- **Stop being the expert on all things.** When you do not understand or do not know, ask students to respond or suggest. This action not only stimulates students' abilities in description, explanation, and clarification but also allows you to model an appropriate technique should students not know or understand a question or response.

- **Take time to write statements on the board or diagram the flow of the discussion to give students a chance to think about it** (Ennis 2000b). As with brain-compatible strategies, diagramming can help organize thoughts and help students to see connections and relationships. Diagramming also suspends the verbal discourse to allow students to collect their thoughts, review the discussion, or develop a new thought or response.

- **Teach children how to work effectively in groups.** Group work stimulates higher-order thinking skills more than individual or competitive tasks do (Skon et al. 1981). A problem-solving process can be more effective if students work in small groups and then come together to compare results (Potts 1994). Ocansey (1994)

Students can help each other build thinking skills by working in groups.

also supports the use of small groups to allow students to identify and justify actions and devise ways to solve the problems that they have discovered. If students are to practice thinking skills in group activities, you need to be mindful of the group processes that you need to teach, model, and support. Adequate supervision and intervention in group activities is necessary if you want the entire group to be involved (Rovengno et al. 1995).

- **Allow the use of props to support the thinking process.** Posting the process on the wall, handing out cards containing the essential information for a skill, or allowing students to go to an information station will assist with learning until students master a skill. Allow students to use the teaching aids but gradually wean them away as they gain proficiency. These charts could also assist transfer in a variety of contexts or subject areas (Potts 1994).

Assessing Thinking

Assessment of students' ability to think can be a complex problem. As with other types of learning, students indirectly show evidence of acquisition. Although a number of techniques are possible, both you and the students should agree on what good thinking entails. If possible, testing should take place in authentic, real-life situations. Involving students in the development of assessments addresses thinking skills and helps students buy into the process (Baron 1986).

The content of the assessment must mirror what you are teaching. Finding a ready-made assessment is not always possible, but classroom teachers can be a good resource for examples of assessments. This approach not only links physical education and other academic subject areas but also reduces instruction in the use of the assessment if students are already familiar with it. In most instances, you will have to adapt assessments found in other academic areas or make up your own.

Informal and Formal Assessment

Informal assessment gives you a general idea of what students know in relation to the skills taught. You might do informal assessment during the course of a class by posing questions to individuals, groups, or the class as a whole. You would use the information gained primarily to help you decide how to structure the next class.

Formal assessment usually has written criteria and clear levels of performance. The scope of the assessment is more limited to the direct evaluation of a specific skill or process and results in a score or grade. The assessment could be either a product or a process measure that represents proficiency or achievement. You, the individual student, or a peer can obtain the assessment information in written, oral, or action form. The assessment should take place in a situation that is as authentic as possible.

Developing Tools to Assess Thinking

In most instances you will find it advantageous to develop your own assessments so that you can match them to the students' ability levels and the content of the lessons presented. You may be able to adapt assessment rubrics or tools from other academic areas or levels to meet your specific needs. A well laid out curricular model will help greatly in this process.

1. **Clearly define the thinking skills or processes to be assessed.** Determine the steps in the process if you will be assessing a specialized thinking skill.

2. **Identify how students in physical education could demonstrate skills or processes.** The thinking skills must be matched with observable behaviors demonstrated by the students which show acquisition of the thinking skills. For example, planning how the

steps of the process must be listed will show that the student has acquired the thinking process.

3. **Develop an assessment rubric.** Identify what a competent (average) level of expertise would be for demonstrating each skill and then further define higher and lower levels of accomplishment. Try out the rubric and adjust as necessary. Introduce it to the students.

Developing Assessment Tasks

After determining what you are looking for to assess the thinking process, the next step is to develop the actual tool or task to yield the assessment. Because assessment must occur while students are active, the tool itself needs to be concise and clear. With the guidance of your criteria, you can observe the process as students apply the thinking or at the end by examining the result of the students' thinking. Following are some types of tasks that you might use.

Open-Ended Questions or Movement Challenges

With this style of assessment you ask students an open-ended question and then assess their response. You will need to try out the questions with the class ahead of time. The questions need to be explicit enough to elicit the desired response. Students follow up their oral or movement response with justification, evidence, or reasons (orally or in writing). You can also identify dispositions from what students reply or show. You observe and record the responses with a checklist or written comments, or you can record the responses with audiotape or videotape for review later. You must be open to responses that may be different from what you expect but meet the criteria for effective use of the underlying thinking process (Norris and Ennis 1989).

Discussion Session

Another technique to assess critical thinking or thinking in general is to pose questions that require thought processes. Allow students time to develop responses and then listen and observe the discussion or movement response. During the discussion use a checklist to check off evidence of processes and make notes on individual students. You or a student could lead the discussion. See figure 2.1 for a sample assessment tool for use in a discussion.

Think-Alouds

After they experience a task or situation, have students tell the process that they used to come up with the task or answer. This style of questioning helps orient students to metacognition (Baron 1986). You could audiotape or videotape the session and review it later.

Discussion Assessment for Critical Thinking

N—No opportunity to show
1—Does not show evidence of the characteristic
3—Often shows evidence of the characteristic
5—Consistently shows evidence of the characteristic

Names	Gives correct content information	Asks for or gives reasons	Treats all participants with respect
Jason			
Bethany			
Erin			
Keesha			
Darrin			
Juan			
Chris			

Figure 2.1   Sample assessment tool for use in a discussion.

The Making of . . .

This technique is similar to Think-Alouds. The difference is that students record the process as they develop a project or complete a task. Groups note and comment on snags and glitches experienced along the way. The assessment could be in written form, or students could make a videotape or audiotape. This technique could also highlight group process skills (Baron 1986).

Movement Tasks or Challenges

Develop a movement task or challenge that requires the desired thinking skill or process and ask students to complete it. The task should be familiar to them. You need to construct the task carefully to allow students to use the thinking process desired and express it in a motor product. View the response and question students to determine the processes that they used. Students could also produce a written response, or you could videotape the task and view it later with the students (Baron 1986). You could also produce a video that all students watch and then respond to in writing or orally by applying the required thinking processes. Another task could be the development of a group project such as the development of a scoring rubric for a gymnastics meet (Woods and Bok 1995).

Written Assessments

You could use written assessments, either alone or in conjunction with other means, in a variety of ways to assess a thinking process. A written test should include less complex mental functions such as recall, but the emphasis should be on having students demonstrate knowledge about how to apply the processes in real game or play situations (Woods and Bok 1995). Videotape or computer simulations to show a situation would be appropriate for students to respond to. Use journaling to assess the processes used by students in response to questions. Students could write a response to a situation that occurs in class (e.g., cheating in a game, group process) or a situation that you design to elicit the thinking skill that you want to assess.

Buell and Whittaker (2001) believe that when students use writing and critical thinking in a particular subject area, the assessment must be taught explicitly to develop content understanding and the ability to reflect on what was learned. If students are to use writing to assess thinking, you need to instruct them in the style and form of writing that you desire and that reflects physical education.

Administering the Assessment

After you design the assessment, you need to give students extensive exposure to the assessment process to allow assessment of the thinking, not the learning of the assessment tool. Allow adequate time for students to address complex tasks. Assessment should occur repeatedly and often to ensure that the information is embedded in long-term memory.

If thinking in physical education settings is to be taught, these skills must also be assessed. Developing a clear, concise, easy-to-use assessment tool will be worth the effort to demonstrate that teaching was effective and that learning has occurred.

CHAPTER 3

Introductory Activities

What Are We Doing Today?

NASPE Standards
2, 5

Intelligence Types
IA, L

Thinking Skills
Identification, discernment, causal reasoning, hypothesis, analysis

Movement Skills
Locomotor skills, or this activity could be used to introduce or focus students before starting the class and to allow students to develop and ask questions.

Equipment
Spread throughout the environment whatever equipment is necessary for the lesson or activity. The equipment will give students clues about the activity of the day. You can add some equipment not related to the lesson to stimulate analysis and problem solving.

Formation
Students sit in front of you or are scattered throughout the space as part of the warm-up.

Description
1. Have students warm up before class by moving around the equipment (or by performing warm-up laps around the perimeter of the activity space) using a specific locomotor skill. As they move, ask them to observe the equipment that is in the space.

2. On a signal, ask students to freeze. Then ask, "Who has a guess or hypothesis about what we are doing in class or in our session today?" Ask students to raise their hands. When called on, students must phrase the response in the form of a question (e.g., "Are we going to play a game today?"). Write the responses (on a whiteboard or flip chart) for students to view. Give feedback or hints if desired.

3. Allow students 10 responses (more or less) to discover as many of the class activities as they can. They can use the 10 responses to guess, or they can ask you questions to gather more information about the activities of the day. Students try to guess as much as they can about the activities for the day.

4. At the end of the session, during cool-down, show students the list of questions and guesses from the beginning of class and ask them how many of the guessed activities they accomplished during that class. Ask them what they did that they did not guess.

5. End the class by asking students what they think they will be doing in the next class.

Movement–Learning Connection

- Use this activity to allow students to activate the parts of the brain needed for learning and to access any memories that they may already have about the tasks for the day.

- Ask students how they decided what questions to ask. What clues in the environment were most helpful? Least helpful? Why?

- Use the activity to engage the students' emotions (excitement, anticipation) to support learning.

- When you play the game the next time, see whether the students can guess the activities in fewer than 10 questions.

- Use questions to prompt appropriate responses and support the formation and asking of questions by the students. This action encourages them to process and formulate responses. Here are some suggestions to stimulate thinking:
  - What is the proper way to ask a question?
  - How did you decide what questions to ask?
  - How did you decide which clues were important?
  - Why did you eliminate that particular clue?
  - Who else has an idea to share?
  - What else are we going to do today?

Story Time 📖

NASPE Standards
1, 2, 5, 6

Intelligence Types
L, IE, K

Thinking Skills
Analysis, synthesis, decision making, elaboration, relating, generalizing

Movement Skills
Whatever is necessary for the story, or you can assign one to include.

Equipment
Props may be helpful. Use short books that the students have previously read or that they could easily read in class.

Formation
Place small groups of four students at stations set up around the gym. Place a short book, photocopies or printouts of short stories, or a series of pictures at each station.

Description
1. Ask students to take turns reading a story or telling a story using the pictures. You may have to cue students when to change reading or telling roles. For example, have each student read a paragraph or a page.
2. Once the story is read or told, ask students to act out the story literally, or to interpret it as they choose, depending on the abilities of the group. For example, an abstract way to act out a story is to ask students to convey the message of the story using just one movement.
3. Place two groups together and let one act out their story while the other group is the audience. Then switch. Rotate groups.

Movement–Learning Connection
- Before students read the story, ask them to guess what the story is about from its title.
- If stress levels rise, break off from the activity and have students stretch to keep emotions at moderate levels.
- If a group cannot come up with ideas, have them move within the gymnasium space (or be active in some manner) to increase circulation to their brains. Then have them regroup.

- To keep emotions positive, ask students to come up with a positive story or a story with a positive message.
- Give students a set of pictures and have them make up a plausible story or mix up the pictures to develop another story.
- Ask what led them to develop a particular story line.
- Ask students what other options they have for a story line.
- Stop the storytelling at some point and ask students to guess what they think will happen next.
- Give students a set time to discuss the story.

Number Write

NASPE Standards
1, 5, 6

Intelligence Types
S, IE, LM

Thinking Skills
Identification, relating, composition, variety, analysis, problem solving

Movement Skills
Students could use walking and other locomotor skills to move into and out of formations. They use nonlocomotor skills to form numbers.

Equipment
Whiteboard and markers or overhead projector (if you choose to write the numbers rather than call them out)

Formation
Students in groups of four to six

Description
1. Call out a number from one to nine, write the number on a whiteboard, or show it on an overhead projector.
2. Students must manipulate their groups into the shape of the number as it would appear when viewed from above. Require that students remain in physical contact with each other (using appropriate touching). A good approach is to have students start by holding hands.

Movement–Learning Connection
- Change the number or orientation of the number (e.g., students could form their numbers as they are oriented on the whiteboard, standing upright in space or if standing behind the number).
- Increase the complexity of the task by placing two groups together and then allowing them to try two-digit numbers (e.g., for the number 29, one group makes the 2 and the other the 9).
- Ask students to form the answer (a number) to a simple math problem or a number answer to a question (e.g., what number is this day in the week?).
- Ask students to form a sequence of numbers (e.g., the school address, their classroom number, the school telephone number) by moving from

one formation to the next. For example, to form the number 911, first they would form a 9, then change the formation into a 1, and finally form a second 1.

- The activity will engage the brain better if the number selected has personal meaning to the students (their year in school, the number of wins that their soccer team has, or their age).
- Changing the position of the performance (e.g., on the floor or standing) forces the brain to stay engaged.
- Allowing two groups to work together increases stimulation for the brain.
- For variety, to keep the brain engaged, try letters of the alphabet or words.
- Ask the group to come up with some ideas and then develop a plan before trying to make the number. This approach encourages planning and development of a variety of responses.
- Review a simple problem-solving process to assist the students.
- After each attempt, assign one member of the group to give feedback to the group.
- Ask one group to assess the clarity of another group's numbers and give suggestions.

Numbers by Body

NASPE Standards
1, 5, 6

Intelligence Types
LM, IE, K

Thinking Skills
Relating, ordering, novelty, identification

Movement Skills
Bending and twisting (e.g., nonlocomotor skills), relationships with others

Equipment
Cards with numbers or a board to write numbers on

Formation
Groups according to the size of the number to be formed (e.g., group of three for the number 194)

Description
1. Predetermined groups move in general space (e.g., side by side, single file, in the shape of a triangle) as directed by you. You could also form groups by asking students to form groups of a particular size (e.g., "By the time I count to three, form a group of three for the next number").
2. On a signal, hand out a card, call out a number, or have each group pick up a card from the floor. Each group of students identifies and then forms a series of numbers according to the number of digits in the number given (e.g., 194). They then form the number with their bodies (one student forms a 1, one forms a 9, and the third forms a 4).

Movement–Learning Connection
- To keep the brain engaged, have students perform the number backward, top to bottom, or from smallest to largest.
- After students have some success with the task, time the groups to see how long it takes them to form a number. Offering a time challenge is not appropriate unless students have learned the task well and all can perform it without needing time to process the task cognitively. Ask students to beat their previous record. Be mindful of the effect of increased emotion on performance.

- Use the number of the area code for your geographic area or another known number to which memories are connected.
- Add variety by adding a student as a decimal point or a comma for larger numbers.
- Place each student in a leadership role by putting her or him in charge of organizing the group to form the number.
- Link the activity with math by having one member of each group record the numbers and then having groups add them up at the end of class.
- Place on each card a problem that the group must solve and then form the answer with their bodies. Designate one of the groups as problem-solvers and have them confirm the answers determined by the groups.
- Acknowledge positive emotional support of others by members of the groups.

Whole-Body Feelings

NASPE Standards
5, 6

Intelligence Types
IA, K

Thinking Skills
Recalling, reflection, clarification, variety, illustrating

Movement Skills
Locomotor and nonlocomotor movement

Equipment
None

Formation
Self-space

Description

1. Identify an emotion and ask students what that emotion looks like (e.g., "How does your face and body look to others when you are angry?"). Model the emotions as needed.

2. Ask students to show the emotion using nonlocomotor movements and facial expressions. For example, for happy, students might bend and extend from a low to a high level with a smile on their faces.

3. Next, ask students to move in general space in a manner depicting the emotions.

Movement–Learning Connection

- Asking students to learn about and express emotions can lead into their recognition of the effect of their emotional level on their ability to learn. High emotion will impair the ability to think.

- Put students in pairs or small groups and have them act out an emotion while other students identify what emotion they are portraying.

- Have students use a group high five or otherwise celebrate (positive emotion) with an appropriate response.

- To keep the brain engaged, ask for a variety of ways to express a single emotion.

- Have students progress from one emotion to its opposite (e.g., sad to happy) in eight counts or beats.

- Ask students how they recognize when a person is angry, happy, sad, or has any other emotion.
- Ask students to identify one characteristic of a particular emotional expression (e.g., "What do the eyes look like or what are the hands doing to show a particular emotion?").
- To stimulate memories, ask students to identify when and where they have felt those emotions in the past. Use the situation to discuss appropriate expression and control of emotions to promote future learning.

Roll a Move

NASPE Standards
1, 5

Intelligence Types
LM, M, IE

Thinking Skills
Recalling, composition, synthesis

Movement Skills
Various dance steps, fitness exercises, game skills, or gymnastic moves

Equipment
- A die for each group
- A chart with the move that corresponds to the number on the die (see sample charts on page 55)

Formation
Groups of three to five students in assigned areas in general space, each area with a chart and a die

Description
1. Each student in the group rolls the die to determine one move that the group will perform as part of the routine. Each number on the die corresponds to a move on a chart or card (e.g., 1 = step-hop, 2 = grapevine step, 3 = turn).
2. After determining the moves, the group puts them together in a sequence or routine. The group practices the routine and develops smooth transitions between the moves.

Movement–Learning Connection
- Ask students to roll the die again to determine how many times they will repeat each move (in a row or in the course of the pattern).
- Prepare a rubric with criteria for performance of the routine to assist students in developing a quality routine.
- Ask students to change the start and end points of their routines (e.g., ask them to perform their routine from move 3 to the beginning or from the end to the beginning).

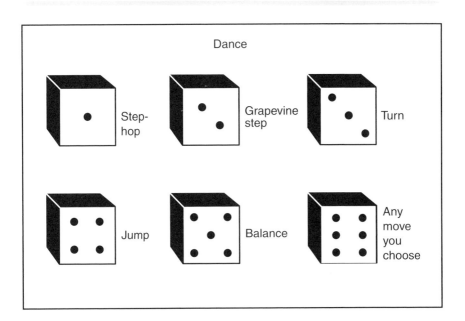

Dance

Step-hop

Grapevine step

Turn

Jump

Balance

Any move you choose

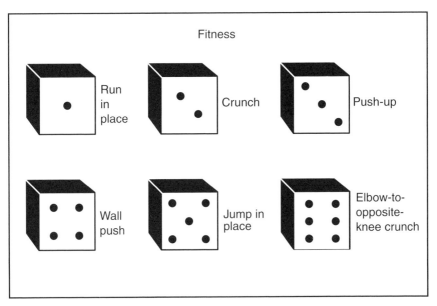

Fitness

Run in place

Crunch

Push-up

Wall push

Jump in place

Elbow-to-opposite-knee crunch

(continued)

Roll a Move (continued)

- Allow students to perform their routines three groups at a time to decrease the anxiety that some may feel performing in front of others.

- Give students a blank poster and have them develop a chart that relates a movement to the number on the die. For example, in basketball, 1 = jump shot, 2 = baseline cut, 3 = bounce pass, and so on. Another group of students would then use the chart to develop player movement or an offensive play.

- To simulate memories, ask students to identify board games that use dice (e.g., Monopoly).

- Ask each group to give their movement sequence a name.

- Give students a list of three routines and ask them to perform them in a series.

- Ask each group to teach another group their routine.

- Combine groups and have the groups link the two routines together.

- Ask how group members supported each other's ideas.

- Ask groups how they determined the order of the moves or the transitions between moves.

Contribution Fitness

NASPE Standards
1, 4, 5

Intelligence Types
K, IE, M

Thinking Skills
Recalling, analysis

Movement Skills
Any movements or exercises that could be repeated for a period of time or for a set number of repetitions (e.g., push-ups, balls volleyed to the wall, rope jumping, grapevine steps)

Equipment
- Equipment as needed for the stations
- A colored piece of paper with places designated on it for the teams to record the number of exercises completed at each station
- Markers or writing implements

Formation
Five or more members on a team with enough stations so that each team could be at a different station. More stations than number of team members is preferred.

Description
1. Select teams and identify them by color. Identify teams in some manner so that team members can record their performance on their team's sheet of paper posted at each station.
2. One member of each team goes to a different station. (See sample stations on page 58.)
3. On a signal, have students perform the activity that is posted at their respective stations for a set period (e.g., 30 seconds).
4. When the time ends they record the number of completed repetitions on their team's recording form (identified by color) and set up the station for the next group (e.g., put equipment back in its starting place, return markers to the box, etc).
5. When instructed to do so, group members then move to the next station to complete another task.
6. At the end of class, each team collects its recording forms and adds up the team repetitions for each team member at each station.

(continued)

Contribution Fitness (continued)

Sample Fitness Stations

1. **Jump rope.** Count the number of single jumps completed.

2. **Abdominal crunch.** Lie on your back, bend your knees, and cross your arms on your chest. As you contract your stomach muscles and bring your shoulders off the floor, reach out with your elbows to touch your thighs. This counts as one crunch. Count the number completed. Rest if you need to, then continue your count.

3. **Half push-ups.** In a full push-up position, drop down half the distance to the floor and return to the start position. Count the number of repetitions you complete.

4. **Superhero hold.** Lie on your stomach, lift your legs and arms off the ground, and hold. Keep track of how many seconds you are able to hold the position without lowering the limbs. If you need to, rest and then start again. Keep a total count of the time spent in the superhero hold.

5. **Head-to-toe push-up.** In push-up position, hold your weight with one (right) arm while completing this touch sequence with the other arm (left): Touch your head, opposite shoulder, same side hip and the outside of the thigh; that's 1. Repeat with the other arm (right) while supported (by the left arm); that's 2. Rest if you need to, then start again.

6. **One-arm wall push.** Stand at arm's length from the wall. Place one hand on the wall about at the level of your sternum. Place your other hand on your arm at the elbow. Flex the arm on the wall and bring the opposite elbow close to the wall, then extend the arm back to the starting position. This counts as one repetition. When you get tired, do it with the other arm.

7. **Arch-out abdominal crunch.** Lie on your back with your fingertips under the arch in your back. Bend your knees. Contract the abdominal muscles to bring your back down to touch your fingers. One contraction counts as one repetition.

Movement–Learning Connection

- Teams could add up their repetitions to see how many total repetitions they performed.
- Ask students to develop individual and group goals for improvement. Allow students to strategize how they might improve their totals.

- Students could assess their individual performance against data collected in the past. Use the data as an assessment or in math problems.
- Watch out for children's tendency to want to be the best, which may result in inflated numbers. Ask why a student might do this. Ask whether inflating numbers is the right thing to do.
- Allow a drink station. The brain needs water to work.
- Discuss how individual effort combined with the work of others increases the amount of work completed.
- Support individual students' efforts to improve fitness levels.
- Recognize students who positively support their teams.

Jump the Line

NASPE Standards

1

Intelligence Types

N, K, L

Thinking Skills

Recalling, relating, classification, decision making

Movement Skills

Jumping to the side and back or other locomotor patterns

Equipment

None

Formation

Students stand one behind another along a line on the floor with their sides to the line, facing you.

Description

1. Identify which side of the line is one term (e.g., puddle) and which side is the other term (e.g., sidewalk).
2. When you call out, "Puddle" or "Sidewalk," students jump over the line or stay where they are, depending on the command. You may have to hold a sign or a picture oriented on the correct side for students to view.
3. If students make a mistake they realign themselves on the correct side and continue playing.

Movement–Learning Connection

- Change the word commands (e.g., "The right side is now 'two-step,' and the left side is now 'grapevine'").
- Use a characteristic of the term rather than the word (e.g., "hard" for sidewalk, and "wet" for puddle).
- Ask students how they remembered which side was which.
- Use relaxation exercises between games if students become too excited. Ask students to take deep breaths or perform some crossing-the-midline exercises (see page 12) to get ready for the next command.

- Use terms covered in class (e.g., the right side could be "dribble," and the left side could be "pass"). Help students learn which side to jump to by using an association (e.g., "What hand do you dribble a basketball with? If you use the right hand, use that as a clue to help you remember to jump to the right when you hear the word 'dribble'"). Ask students what other association might work for them or what association a person who is left-handed could use.

- Use other academic content. Label one side as "odd" and the other as "even" and then give students a math problem to solve before jumping. Or label one side as "healthy" and the other as "not healthy" and then call out a snack food (e.g., potato chips, apples). Students must jump to the side that they think is correct.

Spelling B-Line

NASPE Standards
1, 2, 5

Intelligence Types
L, IE, K

Thinking Skills
Recalling, analysis, decision making, relating

Movement Skills
Various locomotor skills

Equipment
List of spelling words and locomotor skills (see example below)

Spelling Word	Locomotor Skill
Guard	Slide step (5 times)
Foul	Jump straight up with arms extended over head (4 times)
Violation	Cross or scissors step (9 times)
Goal	Run three steps, get low to stop a rolling ball (as a goalie) (4 times)
Throw in	Run three steps, perform a throw-in motion (7 times)

Formation
Divide the class into groups of three or four. Position the groups behind a start line and identify a finish line across a space. (See diagram on page 63.)

Description
1. Give each group a list of spelling words and a locomotor movement for each word, such as the one shown above (e.g., (1) Spell "think" using hopping; (2) spell "memory" while skipping). Each group should have the same list.
2. Let the groups practice by spelling each word and executing its corresponding locomotor movement five times. Students should move in unison with their groups (standing shoulder to shoulder) from the start line to the finish line and back until they have practiced all the words.

3. After the practice period, line all students up along the start line. Tell students that on your signal, all groups will spell each word as they move in unison from the start line toward the finish, stopping when they have finished the word. To begin, have students assume the push-up position (weight on the hands with the body off the ground) in a circle with their heads toward the center of the circle (see diagram). Groups will start each spelling sequence in push-up position, get up, move and spell, and then return to the push-up position.

4. Call out a word (e.g., "think") or the movement (e.g., "hop") to the class, all of whom are waiting in push-up position. If you call out "hop," students must remember which word is linked with the word "hop" and spell that word (e.g., "think") while hopping once for each letter (in this case, five times). In the same way, if you call out the spelling word, they have to remember which locomotor movement is attached to that word.

5. Listen for correct spelling as students move across the floor.

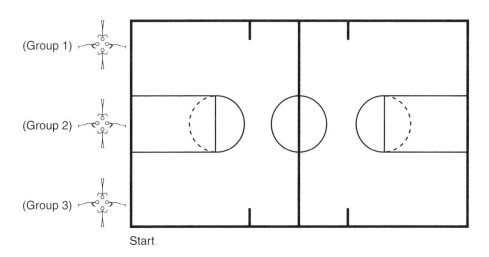

Start

Movement–Learning Connection

- Adding movement to cognitive processing gives the brain another means to access the information, so ask students questions relating to the movements that they practiced (e.g., "What word did we hop to spell? Now spell that word for me").
- Add variety and keep the brain engaged by repeating the activity with new words that the group has not practiced, or have students spell the words backward while moving backward.

(continued)

Spelling B-Line (continued)

- During the closure of the lesson ask volunteers to spell the words learned in the lesson.
- Ask students to practice spelling by having the entire class spell the words in unison.
- Add some stimulation or emotion by asking the groups, when you give them a new or already learned word, to confer (in push-up position) and to stand up, shoulder to shoulder, if their group can spell the word. On command, the groups who are standing spell out the word (e.g., "equilibrium") in unison, moving one skill repetition per letter as directed. Groups can pass on spelling if they choose and not move. Listen to and monitor the groups who have elected to spell. If you hear an error, stop that group at the point of the error. After all groups have completed spelling and have moved toward the finish line, ask one group to spell the word again to reinforce correct spelling.
- Add an element of competition by allowing the group who crosses the finish line first to be the winners for that round.
- Ask a student if the word is correct. Ask how the student knows that.
- Ask a group to define the word or act it out (e.g., "Show me 'equilibrium'").
- Ask groups to recall words used in previous turns.
- Allow students to spell in unison to practice difficult words.
- Use a word repeatedly to support the formation of a memory.
- Have groups make a sentence or a movement sequence using the term after they have spelled it (e.g., hop for each letter of the word "swing" and then finish by swinging a body part).
- Keep the game active by having students move at a brisk pace but allow sufficient time for thinking.
- Use the activity to introduce or review words that will be used in class that day, or that were used in past classes, to allow students to assemble memories.
- Increase practice opportunities by having individual groups work with a list of words and movements. Assign one student as a spell-checker (with the list and correct spellings) to give feedback as needed. Change this position often.

Fact or Fiction Fitness

NASPE Standards
1, 2

Intelligence Types
K, I, L

Thinking Skills
Comparison and contrast, justification, clarification, discernment

Movement Skills
Fitness exercises

Equipment
None, but could use equipment to show skill execution as part of the question

Formation
Students scattered in general space in positions where they can see you

Description
1. Using class content, state a "fact or fiction" statement in relation to what you have taught.
2. If students believe the statement to be a fact, they perform one exercise (e.g., abdominal crunches). If they believe that the statement is fiction, they perform another exercise (e.g., alternate shoulder touches while in push-up position). Each student must select fact or fiction and perform the chosen exercise a set number of times.
3. After students complete the exercise, ask two students each to give a reason why he or she believes the statement to be fact and then ask two others why they think that the statement is fiction.
4. Give the correct response and then ask another question.

Movement–Learning Connection
- Ask more than one student to respond before giving the answer.
- Give students time to come up with a reason.
- You could demonstrate motor skills and ask students whether your performance was correct. Ask students to correct the skill execution or show a better way to move.
- Use a show-of-hands vote and ask one student to count the votes.
- When a student gives an incorrect answer, use crossing-the-midline exercises to get the students' brains working.
- Play this game during a fitness run or walk. Have students jog. After asking students to stop jogging, state the fact-or-fiction statement.

Nature Run

NASPE Standards
1, 5

Intelligence Types
N, S, IA, K

Thinking Skills
Recalling, ordering, comparison and contrast

Movement Skills
Locomotor skills, pathways

Equipment
Labels, pictures, or actual items from nature

Formation
Individual students or small groups begin in a start area. Conduct the activity in a large space with nature items arranged within it. An area outside would be best because you could use trees or other objects in the environment. If you play inside, post pictures of nature items on the walls or on cones on the gym floor.

Description
1. Identify items in nature in the surroundings (grass areas, flower bed, different trees, gravel, and so on) and choose several to use in the game. Prepare cards that list the chosen environmental objects and a corresponding number (see sample cards on page 67). Prepare enough cards for each student to have one card. Make up five to ten extras to have enough to keep the game going. Cards should have the items in the environment ordered in a variety of ways (e.g., card one has 1. Oak tree, 2. Dandelions, 3. Small bush, then card two has 1. Geraniums, 2. Maple tree, 3. Prairie grass, 4. Pine straw, and so on).

2. Give a card to each student or group. Students must run (or move in a prescribed manner) to the first item listed on the card, then to the next, and so on until they have completed the path by traveling to each environmental item and then returning to the start. Students or groups start with different cards so that different students or groups are going to different nature objects.

3. After finishing a card, students or groups turn in the old card, obtain a new card, and go again. Several groups can be moving in the space at the same time. Caution students to watch out for one another. You may need to mark the environmental items with numbers or names initially to help students.

Movement–Learning Connection

- Ask students to create a card for a peer.
- Ask students to answer a question or read about nature at each location before moving to the next.
- Ask students to draw the pathway that they just completed on a piece of paper or draw each "leg" as they complete it prior to beginning the next.
- Initiate a discussion of safety issues in relation to this game (e.g., fire ants, watching where they are going).
- Use pedometers and allow students to estimate the number of steps in the pathway on their cards.
- Keep students moving. Have each group keep track of the number of cards that they completed or challenge them to complete five trips.
- Have a variety of cards with interesting pathways.
- To improve fitness benefits, ask students to link the pathways of two cards and jog the entire (combined) pathway.
- Have students perform the path backward or in another order (3, 1, 4, 2).
- Instead of giving the destinations, identify some features in the environment (e.g., school wall, parking lot, climbing structure) on a card to help orient the students. The path on the card is drawn in relation to the features in the environment. Each leg of the path has a number of steps assigned to it (e.g., 22). The students move 22 steps and then identify a nature item close to where they ended their 22 steps. The students then write the item on the card.

Activity based on Hinson 1995.

Sample Cards for Nature Run

Card A

1. Group of three pine trees
2. Single oak tree
3. Flower bed by gymnasium door
4. Small bush by the playground gate
5. A patch of at least six dandelions

Card B

1. Maple tree
2. Path between two buildings
3. A spot with at least six pinecones
4. Tall grass or weeds
5. A rock the size of your hand

Jump Your Partner's Height

NASPE Standards
1, 2, 5

Intelligence Types
LM, K, S, IE

Thinking Skills
Application, hypothesis, clarity, relating

Movement Skills
Jumping or any locomotor skill

Equipment
- Beanbags or markers
- Lines or markers on the floor

Formation
Partners spread in general space

Description
1. Have students start standing behind a line or marker. Ask them to estimate how many jumps (or other movements) they would need to perform to match their partner's height.
2. Ask students to jump the distance or number that they estimated. The jumper or the partner places a beanbag at that end point.
3. After the jumps have been marked, the partner lies down with her or his feet at the starting point to see how close the beanbag or marker is to her or his head. The partners switch, and the other partner jumps.

Movement–Learning Connection
- Ask students how they came up with their estimates.
- Ask students to show how far they were over or under by showing that distance between the palms of their hands.
- Ask students how they would help a friend estimate the number of movements to a given spot (e.g., the free-throw line).
- Ask students when they would ever need to use this ability (to estimate the distance that they need to move).
- To add variety, have students try the task with a different motor skill (e.g., heel-to-toe steps, strides).

- Use a locomotor pattern that would make students report the distance in fractions (e.g., two and two-thirds strides).
- To keep the activity positive, ask students to give themselves a pat on the back when they get it right.
- Ask students to give positive feedback to their partners.
- Ask students to try new and unique locomotor patterns to measure the distance (e.g., crab walks, log rolls).
- Instead of having students use locomotor patterns, give them a piece of equipment (e.g., a hockey stick or flying disk) and ask them to estimate how many lengths or widths of the equipment it would take to match the height of the partner.
- To add variety or challenge, have students pick out a point in the space (e.g., the red line) and estimate how many widths or lengths of the equipment it would take to reach that spot. The closest estimate earns a point.

Movement Questions

NASPE Standards
1, 2

Intelligence Types
L, K

Thinking Skills
Identification, hypothesis, focus

Movement Skills
Can be used with any skill, with or without equipment

Equipment
None necessary but can be used with equipment

Formation
Students are spread out in general space.

Description
1. Demonstrate a movement (e.g., a lunge).
2. When a student knows what it is, he or she joins in and does the movement with you.
3. When all or most of the students are participating, you call out, "Who has a question?" At this point students stop moving.
4. Ask a student to identify the movement but to do so in the form of a question (e.g., "What is a lunge?").
5. Demonstrate another movement or have the student who asked the question perform the next movement.
6. Add movement concepts or qualities. Students again must identify the movement in the form of a question (e.g., "What is a lunge performed at slow speed?"). Other sport-related or dance skills could be demonstrated and identified.

Movement–Learning Connection
- You should model the appropriate way to ask questions (e.g., tone of voice; in this case begin with the words "What is").
- Ask students what thinking skill they are using.
- Ask students to classify movements according to characteristics.
- Change the criteria for students' responses. For example, instead of a question the answer must include an adverb or preposition.

- Instead of identifying the skill, students must phrase the answer to ask the function or use of the demonstrated skill or the category the exercise of fitness relates to (e.g., "What is a flexibility exercise?" or "How is a ball passed to another player?").
- Reverse the activity. Ask the question and have students "answer" with the movement.
- Give all students the opportunity to ask a question or perform the movement.
- Increase the complexity of the movements by having students link more than one movement together in a dance step or sequence.
- After students answer, have them ask you a question about the movement to give them practice asking questions.

CHAPTER 4

Basic Activities

As the Wind Blows

NASPE Standards
1, 5, 6

Intelligence Types
N, K, L

Thinking Skills
Identification, novelty, relating, causal reasoning

Movement Skills
Creative movement, locomotor or nonlocomotor skills

Equipment
Signs posted to denote the directions east, west, north, and south

Formation
Students spread in general space or in small groups

Description
1. Have students imagine themselves as leaves floating freely through the air, moving through their environment until you or a student announces, "There's a change in the weather. The wind is blowing to the south."
2. At this signal, all students start moving toward the south, as a leaf blowing in the wind.
3. The wind could be blowing *from* the south as well, which would mean movement toward the north.
4. You can change the manner in which students move toward a specific direction:
   - Hurricane—move around the gym in a big circle.
   - Dust Devil—spin slowly (don't let them get dizzy!).
   - Calm—stop and freeze.
   - Lightning—move in a zigzag pathway.
   - Gusty winds—accelerate and then slow down.

Movement–Learning Connection
- Add variety by using southwest or northeast as the direction.
- Assign students to small groups and have them form their groups into their impressions of a boat, car, or animal. The students must move as a group in the direction given.

- Before students move, ask them to suggest a variety of ways in which to move. Let them select their favorite and tell why.
- After you give a category (e.g., animal, flexibility, or speeds), let students develop a way to move in the desired direction in a manner representative of that category (e.g., elephants moving north).
- Take the signs off the walls and try the game without them. Add a thunderstorm or a snow shower as nonlocomotor movements before the wind blows, or have the shower move in the designated direction (thunderstorms developing in the east and moving toward the west).
- Teach about weather patterns as part of the lesson.
- Use a set pattern of direction. Ask students whether they can identify a pattern in the directions that you have called out.

Paper, Scissors, Stone Tag

NASPE Standards
1, 5

Intelligence Types
K, S, IE

Thinking Skills
Comparison and contrast, clarification, classification, conditional reasoning

Movement Skills
Body control, stopping and starting, running or other locomotor skills

Equipment
None

Formation
Divide the class into two teams (or divide the class into smaller groups to have more than one game going on at a time). Draw two parallel lines on the floor about 10 feet (3 meters) apart to separate the groups. Draw another line behind each group to designate a safe, or no-tag, area for each team. Thirty or so feet (10 meters) behind each team is a finish line, behind which is a safe or no-tag area for each team. Opponents line up along a parallel line facing each other at a distance of 10 feet (3 meters) or more to start. Adjust the space as needed to allow students to turn, run, chase, and be tagged safely. (See diagram on page 77.)

Description
1. Each group has a safe area (no-tag zone) behind the finish line and a meeting area (in the center of the space, along a line).

2. Before moving to the center meeting area, each group meets to decide what sign they will throw—paper, scissors, or stone. The sign for paper is both hands held in front of the body flat with palms up. The sign for scissors is both arms touching at the elbows, palms facing each other—the forearms are moved in opposition to each other like blades of scissors. The sign for stone is two hands clasped together.

3. Members of both groups call out, "Scissors, paper, stone, one, two, three."

4. On three, both groups show their sign. Depending on the sign, one group becomes the chasers and the other the runners.
   - Paper covers stone, so stone runs and paper chases.
   - Stone bends scissors, so scissors run and stone chases.
   - Scissors cut paper, so paper runs and scissors chases.

5. The runners attempt to cross the line and reach their safe zone area before they are tagged. A runner who is tagged joins the other team, and the game continues.

Movement–Learning Connection

- Vary the signals to initiate the chase. For example, three sports that start with the letter *F* are flag football, fencing, and field hockey. State that flag football beats fencing, fencing beats field hockey, and field hockey beats flag football. Assign a movement to each sport (e.g., fencing could be a lunge, field hockey a push pass, and flag football a forward pass). To play the game, each group must show the movement for the sport they choose. Depending on the sport, the chase begins.

- Initiate a debate on the best football teams. Lions beat Cardinals. Cardinals beat Bison. Bison beat Lions.

- Each group selects an animal to mimic. Ask students to come up with categories.

- Instead of giving a signal to initiate the chase, designate each side as a category (e.g., odd or even numbers, aerobic or strength exercises, words that start with a vowel or a consonant). If the problem, number, or word belongs in the category of one of the lines, that line becomes the chasers. For example, you could give a math problem for students to solve and determine as even or odd. If the answer is odd, the odd side chases. In another example, if you call out, "Running," the aerobic line chases the strength line.

- Have students take a deep breath before starting each round.

- To call up memories, ask if anyone has played this game before.

- Ask students to explain what they think is going to happen next as you explain the game.

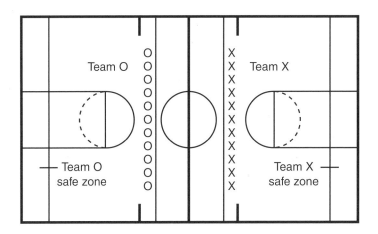

Major Graph

NASPE Standards

2, 5

Intelligence Types

LM, S, IE, K

Thinking Skills

Identification, problem solving

Movement Skills

Walking, locomotor skills on the spots

Equipment

- Equal numbers of numbered cones or spots along the length and width of a gym space to form the *x* and *y* axes (see diagram on page 79)
- Cards with *x* and *y* coordinates on them
- Colored pinnies to identify groups, if desired

Formation

One or a number of areas with students in groups of three to five

Description

1. Give cards with *x* and *y* coordinates to all but one member of each group.
2. Students with cards find their places on the large floor graph and hold the cards in front of themselves. The final member of the group, the checker, starts at 0 and jogs to each student to check the coordinates.
3. After the checker verifies that the coordinates are correct, the student at that location jogs behind the checker to the next data point. When all points have been verified or corrected, the entire group jogs back to 0, obtains a new set of cards, and designates a new checker.

Movement–Learning Connection

- After the students leave the floor graph, ask them to run the path of the line from memory. Have them run the path five times before starting again.
- The placement of students on the graph could form a letter, shape, or number that the group has to identify by viewing the completed graph. Groups could place markers (plastic cones or spots) to mark the locations of their coordinates. Now ask the entire group to run the line of data points, starting at 0 until the last point and repeating a number of times.

- Add jump ropes to connect the dots.
- Ask more than one group to work on one graph to see how their lines intersect or run parallel. Ask students to identify the relationship between the lines.
- Assign each line of data points a variable (y = weight, x = percent body fat). Have students interpret what the information on the graph tells them about the variables (e.g., as weight increases, body fat increases).
- While the students are on the spots (coordinates) have them clear their brains for the next coordinates by performing a series of slow stretches.

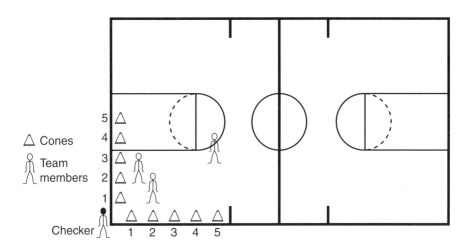

Mural, Mural, on the Wall

NASPE Standards
1, 2, 5, 6

Intelligence Types
K, S

Thinking Skills
Comparison and contrast, view from a variety of perspectives, novelty, composition, generalizing, discernment

Movement Skills
Body control, nonlocomotor movements

Equipment
- Objects to place in the environment that students will use to support production of the picture (e.g., balls, jump ropes, stretch bands, plastic baseball bats).
- Scrap paper and pencils.
- Large posters or pictures of interesting composition for students to interpret. These pictures could relate to what students are studying in the classroom or be products of an art lesson.
- A process or list of questions to be answered to support the thinking process, mounted on the wall.

Formation
Individual or groups of three to five

Description
1. Post the artwork (posters, murals, paintings) on walls or mount them on easels around the activity space.
2. After placing students into groups, send each group to a picture. At that station, students discuss the picture, identify the defining elements of the picture (e.g., shapes, structures, colors), and then attempt to construct a representation of that picture with their bodies and any equipment or props that they think would assist in their representation. Allow sufficient time to obtain a quality response. The number of pictures should exceed the number of groups so that faster working groups can move on to another station after they have completed the first one.
3. When a group is satisfied with their representation, they diagram or sketch their representation on a piece of paper (or each student can do his or her own) and move on to a new picture.

4. At the end of class, ask students to display their groups' interpretations of the artwork. Students can show their drawings and then show their representations. Alternatively, tell students that they are going to be displaying their work in an art gallery and that each group will show one picture.

Movement–Learning Connection

- Ask students to tell why they depicted the pictures as they did.
- Ask students what they think they are doing today.
- Ask students what process their groups used to come up with their designs.
- Ask students to identify the details that they included in their representations. Ask why they included those and not others.
- Ask what they think might have been going on before what is depicted or what could have happened right afterward.
- Use a digital camera to record one of each group's products.
- Ask the groups to compare and contrast their pictures with the originals.
- Use pictures that have positive emotional content.

Bone Volley

NASPE Standards
1, 2, 5

Intelligence Types
N, K, IA, IE

Thinking Skills
Identification, analysis, ordering, focus

Movement Skills
Volleying a balloon or slow-moving ball. Skilled students could use a real volleyball.

Formation
Individual or small group

Equipment
- One balloon or slow-moving ball per student. (If you don't have enough balls for every student to have one, put students in small groups to share the equipment.)
- List of names of bones and muscles or a chart available to each student.

Description
1. Ask students to practice volleying (or bouncing) the balloon off a variety of body parts.
2. Instruct students to volley the balloon off a particular bone (e.g., humerus). To keep the balloon in the air, students should contact the balloon only with the specific bone. Change the bones often to challenge the students.
3. Ask students to volley the balloon alternately off two different bones (e.g., frontal (forehead) bone and then tibia). Add other bones and have students contact the balloon in order (e.g., forehead, clavicle, radius, tibia, metatarsal).
4. For a small group, students could alternately strike the balloon on the specified bone, or one player could call out the bone for the others to strike. Each member could strike different bones in a series (e.g., person one strikes the humerus, person two strikes the tibia, person three strikes the carpals, person four strikes the scapula). The group would work together to complete the series.

Movement–Learning Connection
- Ask what is a part and what is the whole.
- Ask students for suggestions of other bones to use.

- Have students give one reason why this activity is hard or easy for them.
- Have students try contacting bones a number of times in a row before changing to a different bone.
- Use muscles instead of bones.
- Ask students if they can contact a different bone each time they contact the balloon.
- Have students call out the name of the bone they are contacting.

Stretch Band Shapes

NASPE Standards
1, 2, 5, 6

Intelligence Types
S, K, L

Thinking Skills
Identification, application, variety

Movement Skills
Body control

Equipment
- Long jump ropes, stretch bands, or large circles of elastic
- Overhead projector or whiteboard

Formation
Small groups in general space

Description
1. Show the class a shape (e.g., tree, quadrangle, number, star) on a card or whiteboard or project the image on a wall.
2. Have students identify the shape or picture.
3. Ask the groups to form the shape shown with their bodies while using rope or stretch bands as the outside line or perimeter of the shape.

Movement–Learning Connection
- Ask students what information is important to performing this task.
- Have students work together to check whether each other's shapes are accurate.
- Show students a new (different) shape and ask, "How is your shape like this one? Different from this one?"
- Ask students to make their shapes move, shrink, wiggle, and so forth.
- Have students try to make the shape with a partner.
- Show a picture, have each group identify a shape or object, and then have the groups reproduce the shapes or objects in the picture, placing them in relationship with the other groups' objects or shapes as shown in the picture.

Play by Play 📖

NASPE Standards
1, 2, 6

Intelligence Types
L, IE, IA

Thinking Skills
Recalling, recognizing patterns, analysis, objective observation

Movement Skills
Various, depending on the game

Equipment
Whatever equipment is necessary, depending on the content

Formation
An odd number of groups or teams to play small-sided games. The remaining group, called the play-by-play group, is broken up and a member or members are assigned to each game.

Description
1. You or the students review the appropriate skill performance, concepts, or strategies that the play-by-play group will report on (e.g., moving into space, leading the receiver on passes). The teams who are competing go to designated areas to play against each other.
2. Assign one or two members of the play-by-play team to each game.
3. While watching the team or game that they are assigned to, the play-by-play group calls out each time they see an appropriate action or execution: "And there she goes. It's a perfect pass. Look at that execution. She faked before she passed and led the receiver. What a pass!" The play-by-play group can make up their own dialog but must be positive and acknowledge good performance (or whatever you are emphasizing) each time they see it.
4. At the end of the play period, the play-by-play group rotates into a game and another team becomes the play-by-play announcers.

Movement–Learning Connection

- Model or show a video of a sport announcer for the students.
- Allow students to use a list of comments (or script) and then add a critical skill performance element that they could add to the commentary (e.g., "Look at how she takes off on one foot").
- To add variety for older groups, use two announcers, one speaking for each team. Students must keep the feedback positive.
- As teams change, have members of the teams thank the announcers for their positive comments.

The Announcer

NASPE Standards

2, 5, 6

Intelligence Types

L, K, IE

Thinking Skills

Recalling, comparison and contrast, novelty, clarification, discernment

Movement Skills

Whatever skills or concepts you have taught

Equipment

- Depending on the activity, an object that represents a microphone for the announcer to use
- List of content to cover, which can be printed on cards

Formation

Groups in a work space

Description

1. Divide the class into groups of two to five members. Select one member from each group as the announcer.
2. Provide each group a list of thinking skills, movement skills, or other class content that you have taught in previous classes. The group begins with the skill or concept at the top of the page or card.
3. After determining what the term means, the group develops a skit, movement sequence, or representation of the word.
4. After the group determines the movement or action, they develop a script for the announcer. The announcer must be able to describe the movement and give clues to help other students identify the term being represented.
5. After they finish one term, concept, or skill, the group then deals with the second concept on the list. Ask students to change announcers for each group movement.
6. At the end of class, the group shows one of their movements to the class without the announcer. On the second showing, the announcer describes to the audience what is going on without using the term. The audience must guess what the term is.

Movement–Learning Connection

- Allow groups sufficient time to work out the movement with the announcer.
- Ask students to come up with two options for each word.
- Assess group process and help groups learn to work together.
- Require that everyone in the group contribute and then ask individual students what they contributed.
- Have the groups share their work with other groups rather than the whole class.
- If students are uncomfortable about speaking alone, have them work with partners.

Digit Dancer

NASPE Standards
1, 2, 4

Intelligence Types
S, IE, K

Thinking Skills
Recalling, ordering, recognizing patterns

Movement Skills
Hopping and leaping, combinations of fundamental movement patterns

Equipment
- Chalk to put numbers on a sidewalk surface
- Lists of numbers of varying lengths

Formation
The numbers 1 through 10 are written on a 4-foot-by-4-foot (120-centimeter-by-120-centimeter) square surface in random order. Numbers need to be evenly spaced within the confines of the square. (See diagram on page 91.)

Description
1. At each square, one student prepares to read a list of random numbers to the student who is on the square.

2. As one student calls out a number, the student on the square moves as quickly as possible to the number by stepping, hopping, or leaping. Only one foot can be on a number at a time. The reader waits until the active student moves to the number before giving the next number. For each number given, the student on the square must continue to hop on that number until the next number is given.

3. After each student has had a chance to move to 20 different numbers individually, challenge the students by having them jump to numbers in a sequence. Start with one number and add a second. After the student has successfully moved to two numbers in a row, add a third. He or she now moves to the first, second, and then the third number. Add a fourth and so on. When the student can no longer remember the string of numbers to complete the sequence, partners switch roles.

Movement–Learning Connection

- Ask students to hop a certain number of times before they go on to the next number in the sequence.
- Give students a math problem to solve and have them hop to the answer.
- Have students determine the step pattern that they can execute the quickest.
- Ask students to explain how they came up with the best solution.

1	5	8
4	3	9
7	6	2

4 feet

4 feet

- Ask students to perform a contralateral movement at the end of each hop.
- Ask students where they might use an activity such as this one.
- Use the activity to build physical fitness.
- Place the alphabet on the sidewalk and have the students hop to spell words.

PE Summary

NASPE Standards
2

Intelligence Types
K, L, IA

Thinking Skills
Summarizing, generalizing, relating

Movement Skills
Replications of lesson activities

Formation
Mass, group, or individual in general space

Equipment
None

Description

1. At the end of a lesson, ask the class to think of one movement that shows what the class was all about that day. They may not use words. For example, if the lesson was on healthy snacks, jump rope, and a tag game, the students could jump and make a tag motion with one hand while mimicking picking an apple with the other hand.

2. Ask one student to show his or her movement. Ask another student to describe what the first student is demonstrating.

3. Use the students' responses to review the content of the lesson.

Movement–Learning Connection

- Ask a student whether her or his movement represents what the class was about.

- Ask another student to summarize in a few sentences what the other student's movement is saying.

- Have the student complete the statement "This class was like a _____."

- Allow more than one student to show their representations.

- Ask students to tell the best thing that happened to them today in class. Can they show that in a movement?

- Ask students if they recognized any patterns in the class today.

Jump Around the World

NASPE Standards
1, 2

Intelligence Types
S, LM, IE, K

Thinking Skills
Hypothesis, comparison and contrast, application

Movement Skills
Two-footed jumping or other locomotor movement to reinforce your movement curriculum (e.g., heel-to-toe walking, skipping)

Equipment
- Tape (or slotted cones)
- Activity cards, more cards than students to allow freer, safer movement
  - On each card, place a picture and name of a geographical area. Use the major areas of your local region, countries, counties, bodies of water, or the like, depending on what students are studying in other classes. If needed, divide the activity area into two or more subareas and place additional sets of the same cards in these areas. The Internet should provide a wealth of related geographical areas to depict.
  - Add two instructions to each card: (1) next area to travel to and (2) locomotor movement (e.g., hop, walk, skip) to use while traveling to the next area.
- Index card and pencil for each student
- One ruler of any length as a model

Formation
Tape (or slot into cones) the pictures on the floor. Place the pictures (cones) around the activity area. Do the best you can to place each geographical area roughly where it is located in relation to the other areas that you selected. Leave enough space to do the practice activity in step 1.

Description
1. Give each student an index card and a pencil. Have students line up along the long edge of the activity area. Explain that today they are going to estimate how many jumps it will take them to go from one area to the next. (You may also wish to mention the general geographical region that you have selected and why.)

(continued)

Jump Around the World (continued)

2. Selecting a short distance, point out a line (parallel to the line of students) that they are going to practice jumping toward. (Make sure that everyone is the same distance from the line.) Ask them to think of the number of jumps that they think it will take them to cover the distance. Hold up the ruler. Explain that it shows a unit of distance. Emphasize the need to think in terms of jumps of equal length so that each has a personal unit of distance. Then have them record the number that they predict on the index card. Explain that this number is their *estimate*. They should not worry about what another person estimates—everyone jumps differently.

3. Direct students to jump to the line that you have designated, counting their jumps as they travel. Reinforce the need to keep their jumps close to the same length each time. Have students record the actual number of jumps next to their estimated number on the index card.

4. Ask students to signal how closely their estimate came to being correct: If they needed more jumps than they thought, they give a thumbs-up; if they needed fewer, they give a thumbs-down; and if they were exactly correct, they clap for themselves.

5. Now direct students each to find their own geographical location to stand next to in the activity area. Have them look on the card for the next area to travel to, locate it by sight, and then write on the index card their estimate of the number of jumps they will need to get there.

6. Direct students to start jumping and see where they end up. (Continue to encourage students to jump as close to the same distance per jump as possible.) Ask them to identify and write where they are (e.g., Suffolk County, Florida, the Indian Ocean) next to their estimate on the index card. If they are long or short, have them continue toward their target, counting the additional jumps needed.

7. Have all students, successful or not, record the actual number of jumps they needed to get to their destination.

8. Have students take as many trips as time allows. Circulate through the activity area, reminding students to record numbers and locations as directed and to take jumps of the same length.

9. If needed to control behavior, increase safety, and guide students in doing the task correctly, add a signal (music is fun and helps the brain think) to stop and start each round.

Movement–Learning Connection

- List a fact about the geographical area on each card for students to read before moving on. Ask students to tell a neighbor the fact about the area that they have reached before they go on.

- Ask students how they are able to keep their moves the same size. (Note: You may need to supply measuring sticks to help students keep their jumps the same length.)

- Have students, each speaking to a neighbor, identify the areas around the one where they have arrived.

- Ask students to record their path on a map of the region.

- To increase activity, ask students to take a "whirlwind tour" after reaching five areas by jogging around the outside borders of the country before moving to the next area.

- Pair younger or less experienced students. Have one student perform the required movement and the other student record on the index card. Partners switch roles trip by trip.

- Commission older students to make the cards as part of a classroom research project. A group of older students could supply a map of the activity area, providing information for you to set up the cards for other classes.

- Repeat the activity with other geographical regions.

- Safety tips: To help prevent falls, strongly discourage stepping on the cards or cones. Show students how to carry a pencil safely (grasped in a fist with the tip down and just below the pinky finger) to prevent accidentally stabbing oneself or a classmate. Remind students to avoid bumping into other students.

Word Relay 📖

NASPE Standards

1, 2, 5

Intelligence Types

K, L, IE

Thinking Skills

Analysis, composition, identification

Movement Skills

Locomotor skills of choice

Formation

Groups of two, three, or four in relay format

Equipment

- Hoops—one to place the collected letters in and one to travel toward to collect letters
- For younger students, a word wall or list of potential words
- A list of words and cards with the letters of the alphabet on them (see sample list on page 97)

Description

1. After assigning teams, place each group in relay formation at the starting point behind their hoop. A list of terms is at each starting point. Opposite each team is a hoop with the letters of the alphabet on cards in it. (See diagram on page 97.) The cards can be face down or face up. If the cards are face down, students must take the first letter that they touch, not look at each to find the desired letter.
2. Students move (using the locomotor skill that you identify) one at a time (from a starting point to the hoop) to collect one letter of the alphabet.
3. Students continue to collect letters one at time, each taking a turn until the group can form a movement-related word (jump, listen, curl, twist) from their list.
4. After they form a word, students perform the movement a certain number of times until you check the word.
5. The group then continues to travel to their hoop to collect letters to form another word. Students may return letters or keep them and use them to form new words.
6. Each relay could have different words to be developed in their hoops. After a time, have the groups rotate to the next relay spot.

Movement–Learning Connection

- When building words, allow students to use the same letter to form two different words as they would in doing a crossword puzzle.
- Ask students if they could make words that are not on the list from the letters gathered.
- Ask what category the word belongs to.
- Ask students what the word means.
- Place a clue on one of the letters to help identify the word that it is used to spell.
- Do not supply older students with a list. Tell students that all words must relate to a particular topic.
- Have students review the terms and meanings at the beginning of the next class.

Sample List of Words

Walk	High	Speed	Backward	Kick
Run	Medium	Pathways	Sideways	Trap
Jump	Low	Straight	Forward	Pass
Hop	Level	Curved	Force	Corner
Gallop	Fast	Zigzag	Light	Goal
Skip	Slow	Directions	Heavy	Foul

Team 1   Team 2   Team 3   Team 4   Team 5   Team 6   Team 7   Team 8

Hoops where teams place collected letter cards

Hoops with letter cards for teams to collect

If You Design It, We Will Copy It!

NASPE Standards
2, 6

Intelligence Types
S

Thinking Skills
Recalling, recognizing patterns, analysis, comparison and contrast

Movement Skills
Running, bending

Equipment
Set up a cluster of equipment in a particular pattern (have the pattern of equipment drawn on a card) across from a start line.

Formation
Relay formation. A group of three students lines up behind a line ready to run and view an arrangement of equipment. Each group of students has a different arrangement.

Description
1. On a signal, the group moves to the equipment to view the arrangement for 30 seconds and then goes back to the start.
2. One at a time, students go to retrieve a single piece of equipment and bring it back behind their line. The teacher may assign or vary locomotor skills to use as students are getting equipment.
3. After they have gathered all the equipment, students reassemble the arrangement to the best of their ability to match the initial arrangement.
4. Compare the students' arrangement with the picture on the card.

Movement–Learning Connection

- Have each group make a new arrangement before rotating to the next relay spot.
- Ask students what the equipment arrangement reminds them of.
- Ask students to diagram the equipment arrangement first (when all have viewed the card and prior to assembling). Then have them put the diagram away and try to reassemble the pattern. Ask whether it was easier or harder to do it that way. Ask why.
- Have students rate themselves on their accuracy.
- Ask for details.
- Ask students what strategy they used to remember the arrangement.
- Have students view a movement sequence (e.g., video, student performance) instead of equipment. Have each group try to remember the sequence and then perform it.

Stump the Teacher

NASPE Standards

2, 5

Intelligence Types

IA, L

Thinking Skills

Hypothesis, recalling, application, discernment

Movement Skills

Catching and tossing

Equipment

A ball to pass to the student asking the question

Formation

Standing in a semicircle

Description

1. When the ball is tossed to a student, she or he asks you a question about the class content.

2. You answer the question, either correctly or incorrectly.

3. The student asks the class if the answer that you gave is correct or not. The class votes on whether the answer is correct or incorrect. If they think that the answer is correct, they jump up and down and cheer. If they think that the answer is incorrect, they stand in a lunge position and give the thumbs-down sign.

4. After surveying the response of the class, the student who asked the question states whether she or he thinks that the answer is correct or incorrect.

5. You give the correct answer. Those who are incorrect must perform some tasks to help them think better (e.g., relaxation, breathing, crossing-the-midline exercises).

Movement–Learning Connection

- Let students look up answers and bring them to the next class.
- Model appropriate question-answering behavior.
- Ask why the answer is correct or incorrect.
- Demonstrate using time to process by thinking before answering (not blurting out an answer).
- Allow all students to ask a question over the course of the term.
- Give positive feedback for good questions or answers.

Compliment Tag

NASPE Standards
1, 5

Intelligence Types
L, IE

Thinking Skills
Identification, relating, composition, variety

Movement Skills
Locomotor movements and dodging

Formation
Setup for a game of tag with hoops placed around the perimeter of the area

Equipment
- Objects to identify taggers and to tag others (e.g., foam ball)
- Hoops for students who have been tagged to move into

Description
1. Start with one tagger. When students understand how to play the game, add an additional tagger. When a student is tagged during the game, she or he must stand in a hoop.
2. To be freed so that she or he can continue play, the tagged student must give three compliments to classmates who move into his or her area. Then the student is free to rejoin the game. For example, a student might say, "Jasmine, you are running really fast. Juanita, I like the way you dodged around Shahib." The teacher monitors the comments and assists students in developing proper compliments.
3. Change taggers after two to three minutes.

Movement–Learning Connection
- Place in the hoop a list of compliments that students might use.
- For older students, a second runner could join the student in the hoop (safe place). After the student who has entered the hoop gives the tagged person a compliment, both rejoin the game.
- Ask students why they need to make positive comments in real life.
- Model appropriate comments for the students.
- Ask how this behavior makes them feel.
- Change locomotor skills.

Reorder the Class

NASPE Standards
2

Intelligence Types
M, S

Thinking Skills
Hypothesis, analysis, recognizing patterns, ordering

Movement Skills
Various

Formation
The formation the class usually assumes to start a lesson (e.g., sitting in the bleachers or around a circle)

Equipment
Cards with the components of the lesson for the day printed on them (e.g., warm-up, practice drills, play a game, dance, cool-down, lecture, fitness exercises, and so on)

Description
1. Ask students to identify the parts of a typical physical education lesson.
2. Show students the card with the part on it. If they do not guess all the parts, review the remaining cards or parts with them.
3. Mix up the cards and call on individual students to draw a card.
4. The order in which the cards are drawn will be the order in which the class will proceed (e.g., nutrition fact of the day, warm-up, game, skill work).

Movement–Learning Connection
- Keep the brain engaged by reordering the events of the day.
- Ask students why the class is usually ordered the way that it is.
- Have students tell what usually occurs in each segment of class.
- Ask students which format they liked better. Ask an individual student what order he or she would like the class to follow. Ask the student why he or she made that choice.
- Ask how it felt to go through the class in a different order.

Read and Move 📖

NASPE Standards
1, 2, 5, 6

Intelligence Types
L, IE, K

Thinking Skills
Novelty, composition, synthesis, relating, summarizing

Movement Skills
Locomotor or nonlocomotor movements depending on the reading passage

Equipment
Papers or books with passages that contain movement words

Formation
A number of stations spread out in the gym with readings at each station, small groups of three to five

Description
1. Assign each group to a station.
2. At each station is a short reading that a designated member of the group will read. If students have not yet developed reading skills, place a picture at each station for them to interpret.
3. The group discusses the passage and decides how they will move to depict the words being read.
4. The reader reads the passage a number of times while the group practices. When they finish, you can ask one group to show their work and then have the groups rotate to the next station. Assign a new reader for the next station.

Movement–Learning Connection
- Ask students to do the opposite of the passage.
- Ask students to do the story backward.
- Ask students to develop a new ending for the story.
- Ask students to relate the plot to a real situation in their lives.
- Teach students to break the passage into parts.
- Have students begin by exploring what the reading reminds them of.
- If students become stuck, have them perform X moves (see page 12) to engage the brain.
- Let each student have an opportunity to be the director and guide the group in a positive manner.

Adverbs on the Move

NASPE Standards
1, 2, 6

Intelligence Types
L, K

Thinking Skills
Recalling, variety, clarity, application, elaboration

Movement Skills
Locomotor or nonlocomotor skills as desired

Equipment
Cards with adverbs written on them

Formation
Students spread in general space and cards placed face down on the ground

Description
1. Instruct students to move in general space (e.g., jog).
2. On a stop signal, students cease moving and each student picks up a card. They determine how that adverb (e.g., softly, quickly) is instructing them to move.
3. On your signal to go, they continue with the locomotor movement (jog) but must now adjust the movement to express the adverb.

Movement–Learning Connection
- Allow time for students to discuss how they figured out how to move.
- Ask students to be accurate and show contrast from one card (or adverb) to the next.
- Encourage students to ask questions of a peer if they do not understand the term.
- Change locomotor movements often.
- Adverbs could also be applied to nonlocomotor movements.
- Use words that students are studying in their classroom.
- Try some adjectives, such as dark, stormy, red, or angry.
- State a sentence and have the students identify the adverb and move like that adverb.

Move to the Beat

NASPE Standards
1, 2, 6

Intelligence Types
M, IA, K

Thinking Skills
Analysis, variety, recognizing patterns, focus

Movement Skills
Any known movement skill, combination of moves, or short routine. A more complex movement may work better.

Equipment
A drum or noise maker to mark the beat

Formation
Students in general space

Description
1. Identify and review a sport skill, dance, or routine that you previously taught.
2. Ask students to move in slow motion to perform the assigned movement.
3. Now ask students to break the flow of their movement into four parts.
4. Allow students to hear the beat that you will ask them to move to.
5. Instruct students to move one part of the movement per beat.
6. Next ask students to break the movement into six or eight parts or increase or decrease the tempo or speed of the beats. Students may perform the parts at the new rate of movement.

Movement–Learning Connection
- Have students estimate how many beats they will need to complete their move.
- Give just the beat, and ask students for a variety of responses to the same beat (e.g., twisting move, throwing a ball, jumping down from a height).
- Have students determine their best movement pattern to the beat, show it to the group, and give reasons for their choice.
- Have students develop their own rhythms. Allow a group to move in unison using the same movement to the beat.
- Ask students to form small groups and link their movements together. They use the same beat or vary it according to the movement.
- Ask how the different beats made them adjust the movement.

Match the Music

NASPE Standards
2, 3, 4

Intelligence Types
M, IA, K

Thinking Skills
Variety, recalling, recognizing patterns, elaboration

Movement Skills
The usual warm-up or cool-down or a set of exercises

Equipment
- CD player
- Different styles or types of music for each day of class

Formation
Students in usual warm-up positions

Description
1. While they perform the warm-up or cool-down exercises, have students respond during the movement to the beat or style of music playing in the background.
2. Students exercise in response to the beat of the music.
3. Change the music and have the students change their movement.
4. Next play a piece of music and have the students or a group select the exercise that best fits the music and exercise to it (e.g., running music, music better to stretch to).

Movement–Learning Connection
- Ask why it is or is not easier to exercise with music.
- Ask students to identify an exercise that works best with this type of music.
- Ask how the music changes the exercise.
- Ask what music they prefer and why they prefer it to other music.
- Ask how this music makes them feel.
- Ask whether music or activity affects their moods or emotions.

Music in the House

NASPE Standards
1, 6

Intelligence Types
M, IA, K

Thinking Skills
Recalling, focus, application

Movement Skills
Whatever skills the students need to practice

Equipment
- CD player
- Various styles and types of music

Formation
Students in general space

Description
1. Ask students to practice a motor skill while the music is playing.
2. At various times focus students on the music and ask them to adjust their skill practice to fit some aspect of the movement (tempo, beat, volume, tone, feeling).
3. Direct students to continue practicing to their own rhythms.
4. Change the music and ask students to change their movements again to match the music.

Movement–Learning Connection
- Have students try to play a game or perform a routine at the tempo of the music or to the style of the music.
- Ask if playing music makes the movements more difficult? Less? Why?
- Have students suggest a game (or movement) to play to a particular piece of music.
- Ask students to identify a beat or pattern of beats that matches their moves. They could sound out the beat as they practice.
- Change the music often.
- Use music that they will hear later in the school year as a dance.
- Have students give examples of times when they had to move to music. Ask whether they enjoyed it.

CHAPTER 5

Intermediate Activities

Imagine It! 🎨

NASPE Standards
5, 6

Intelligence Types
S, IA, IE

Thinking Skills
Recalling, composition, analysis, novelty, planning, variety

Movement Skills
Various nonlocomotor movements

Equipment
- Cards with pictures on them
- A variety of handheld sports equipment that could be used to construct a structure (held up by students or placed in a pattern on the floor like a sidewalk painting)

Formation
Groups of three to six depending on the complexity of the scenes

Description
1. Scatter the equipment in general space. After placing students in groups, give one student in each group, the director, a picture to view. He or she then describes the picture to the group without showing them the picture. Allow the director 30 to 60 seconds to describe the scene in words only.

2. The group must produce the picture as best as they can from what the artist has said by using the equipment and their bodies. Again, to keep students active, set a time limit on the construction phase. For example, to depict a beach picture, the group might use a ball as the sun and jump ropes as the shoreline. Several students could perform the wave, while others could mimic sea birds, a dolphin or two, and so on.

3. Have students assemble their representation of the picture and then show the original on the overhead.

4. Give each group a new picture with a new director.

Movement–Learning Connection

- Change the perspective by showing a painting done by a cubist or impressionist painter and ask students to produce reproductions in that style.
- Monitor each group to be sure that the groups hear and respect each individual's point of view.
- When students are familiar with the activity, add emotion by placing a limit on production time.
- Start the viewing of the picture as a still life and then ask students to move.
- Ask students to add a beginning (what might have happened before the still picture was taken or completed). Then ask what could have happened after that shot. For example, for the beach scene, families could walk onto the beach and then freeze in place, as they appear in the picture. For what might have happened afterward, students could mimic a storm coming to the beach and all the people and animals leaving.
- Set aside time for students to discuss the result before moving on. Ask students to compare the result with the picture. Have them describe how it is similar or different.
- Use a variety of pictures. Start with photos or realistic drawings and then move to more abstract representations.
- Have students select their best work for a gallery showing at the end of class as a celebration.

Obstacles for Learning

NASPE Standards
1, 4

Intelligence Types
S, K

Thinking Skills
Problem solving, planning

Movement Skills
A variety of exercises or skill development movements

Equipment
- Equipment as desired to form an obstacle course
- Paper and markers to make signs for directions

Formation
Groups of three to six with access to various types of equipment. Groups must set up courses in a specific space.

Description
1. Assign each group to a space and give each a component of fitness or motor skill.
2. Each group must develop an obstacle course within their space, using the available equipment, to address the fitness component (e.g., muscle endurance) or motor skill (e.g., dribble with the hands). Each group must develop directions for the course and use the paper and markers to write signs to help classmates move through the course with a minimum of instruction.
3. Each group perfects their obstacle course.
4. Form new groups by placing one student from each group together on a new team. Assign each new team to one of the developed courses. The student who was a part of the group that originally developed the course briefly explains the course and takes the new group through it. Alternatively, the original groups could rotate from course to course and rely on the instructions at the course to complete it. Students continue to go through the course until it is time to rotate to a new course.

Movement–Learning Connection

- Merge all the courses into one and have students move through the course as a whole class.
- Set up the course as a warm-up for the next class.
- Ask how each course addresses the fitness component or skill.
- Ask students why they used the equipment and exercises or drills that they did in developing the course.
- Have each group use their obstacle course to warm up for participation in their classmates' courses.
- Ask each group to write on paper what they liked best about each course.
- Ask students to give positive feedback to the developers of each course.
- Change the manner in which students move through each course (e.g., end to beginning or mix up the rotation).

Movement Notation

NASPE Standards
2, 5, 6

Intelligence Types
M, L, K, S

Thinking Skills
Recognizing patterns, recalling, elaboration

Movement Skills
Locomotor skills, nonlocomotor skills

Equipment
Signs with music notation or a list to call out, each with a specific skill which is performed for a specific number of counts

Formation
General space, set up like a tag game

Description

1. Students perform a particular type of locomotor or motor skill (e.g., skipping or dribbling the ball with the feet).

2. Students perform the skill assigned at the "count" of the note displayed or called out. The students can move at their own "count" until one of the following notes is called or shown:

   - Quarter note: Tap the ball with the instep for 1 count (quick taps).
   - Half note: Tap the ball forward and do not touch it again with the instep until after 2 counts.
   - Whole note: Tap and let the ball roll for 4 counts before tapping it again.

3. The locomotor skill between the notes could also be assigned a quality of music such as staccato. The dribble would then be quick, short taps of the soccer ball. Other possible qualities are allegro (fast) or crescendo (building from small to large movements).

4. Once the movements model the notes, a "rest" is assigned to tag the notes (dribblers) to give them a break. The "rest" moves freely among the performers and touches them like a tagger would. When tagged, the student must rest, trap the ball, and count to four before she or he can rejoin the game. The tagger changes places with the 10th student whom they tag.

Movement–Learning Connection

- Instead of having students perform one skill repetition per beat of the note (e.g., one kick for each beat), have them take that number of counts to complete a movement (e.g., two counts for a half note versus four counts for a whole note to complete a kick on goal).
- Use musical selections to show differences in sound.
- After students learn the game, set up pictures of notes on cones in the space and have students move to each and perform as instructed to increase practice opportunities and activity time.
- Set up a series of notes in a line and have students move down the line.
- Model the moves and counts for students.
- Support initial learning with a metronome.
- Ask students to identify patterns.

Movement Choices

NASPE Standards

1, 5, 6

Intelligence Types

IA, K, L

Thinking Skills

Goal setting, planning, evaluation, reflection

Movement Skills

Whatever skills are involved in the students' choices. Examples of choices are jump rope, a three-on-three basketball game, a gymnastics run, a tag game, fitness exercises, or a fitness video.

Equipment

- Equipment as needed for the activities allowed
- Writing materials for students

Formation

General space in which activities occur

Description

1. Assemble a list of activities that students can perform in the space available.
2. Ask students to choose three or four of the activities or tasks that they wish to perform. Ask each student to list one to four reasons why he or she made each choice. They can direct their reasons toward the goals of the physical education program or the goals set for the unit (e.g., "To improve my passing or improve my ability to hold a balance").
3. Then ask students to set goals for their participation in each activity and write them down (e.g., "I will make 50 free throws or jump rope 100 times").
4. Students perform the activities and work to achieve their goals during the class period. You may want to set a time limit for each activity and signal when students are to perform a new activity.
5. At the end of the class, allow time for students to assess their goal achievement and choose their activities for the next choice day.

Movement–Learning Connection

- Let students work with partners or in groups and work to achieve goals that they have set together.
- Ask students to prove that they have met their goals.
- Ask students to reflect on the activity and give suggestions for the next choice day.
- Discuss with students how they had to accommodate others in the space provided.
- Ask students to select activities that have personal meaning for them.
- Give positive reinforcement for active participation.
- Allow opportunities for students to drink water.

Category Tag

NASPE Standards
1, 4, 5

Intelligence Types
K, S, IE

Thinking Skills
Comparison and contrast, classification, identification, focus, clarity

Movement Skills
A variety of fitness exercises, running, or other locomotor skills

Equipment
Cards with categories of exercises on them. A code for the exercise to be performed or the exercises themselves could be on the card.

Formation
Groups of three to six. General space for a tag game with an exercise station if needed for safety purposes.

Description
1. After assigning students to groups, give each group member a card that has a category on it (e.g., flexibility exercises, speeds, or square dances). You can vary the categories across the groups. For a class of 25, select five to seven different categories.
2. Ask students in the groups to think of a way in which they could move through space to tell other students what their category is. For example, to suggest flexibility, students could move with arms outstretched; for strength, they could display muscle arms; for aerobic exercise, they could mimic the swing of a runner's arms; for muscle endurance, their arms could perform arm curls. Allow students to practice moving while showing their characteristic.
3. Also, ask students to record on the card an exercise that students could do to improve in that area (e.g., 10 side lunges to stretch the adductor muscles of the thigh).
4. Designate one group (e.g., the flexibility group) as the "exercise changers." Ask students to move in a specified way, such as walking or skipping. All groups move through space using the designated locomotor skill while performing the move characteristic of their category (e.g., the flexibility group walks while performing a shoulder stretch). Those in the "exercise changer" group try to tag students in other groups. Change the locomotor skill often to allow many card exchanges.

5. When a student is tagged, she or he trades cards with the tagger and each performs the other's exercise as indicated on the newly received card. Students can complete the exercises at a station off the playing floor or, if safe, on the spot where they were tagged. The student who was tagged and the tagger switch groups.

Movement–Learning Connection

- Change the categories to a sport or type of dance. Groups must come up with a skill to mimic and a drill to perform.
- Ask students how they can be clearer with their movements to reduce confusion.
- Ask students how they determined whom to chase.
- Ask students to summarize the exercises that they did.
- Ask each group to develop another example of an exercise to do when they are tagged and add that to the card.
- Make sure that all students get a chance to chase and be tagged.
- Emphasize the physical fitness aspects of the activity.
- Add a stress-reduction group as a category.
- Add a second group of "exercise changers" so two groups are chasing.

How I See It

NASPE Standards
5

Intelligence Types
K, IE, IA, S

Thinking Skills
Novelty, variety, composition

Movement Skills
Locomotor and nonlocomotor

Equipment
Pictures of scenes; paintings that depict various emotions, feelings, tones, and so on; one per student

Formation
Each student in general space with a different picture

Description
1. Give each student a picture or drawing and ask all to develop in their general space a series of three to five movements that relate to the picture.
2. Place students in groups of two (numbers or letters for groups could be on the back of the pictures to allow for contrast or similarity).
3. Ask each student to show his or her picture to the partner and instruct the partner in the series of moves. The two then combine their movements into one routine.
4. If desired, you could have each partnership join with another set of partners and combine the two movement routines again (four sets of individual moves).

Movement–Learning Connection

- Ask students how the pictures made them feel.
- Ask students to tell what the picture means to them.
- Ask students to outline the thinking process that they used to develop their parts.
- Ask students to present a rationale for why they put the dance together as they did.
- Put groups together and ask them to give feedback on the dance to make it better.
- Hang the pictures in the gymnasium before and after the day of the activity. Later, select a picture and have the students who worked with it lead their dance as a warm-up.
- Ask the student to discuss how their dances could be used to reduce stress.

Individual Journaling: Question of the Day

NASPE Standards
2, 6

Intelligence Types
L, IA

Thinking Skills
Various, depending on the questions used to elicit a response

Movement Skills
Fine motor, writing, drawing

Equipment
Notebooks and pens or pencils

Formation
In self-space, outside class, at a recording station, or during quiet or open practice times

Description
Students respond to a question or statement that you pose, such as the following:

- Identify how you are feeling about _____.
- What happened today in class that made you _____?
- Have you improved? Give examples.
- Describe a decision that you made in class today. What process did you use to come to your decision?
- Did you meet your goal? Why or why not? Why did you decide on that goal?
- Give a rationale (five reasons) for your success today.
- What activities did we do today that helped you develop your skills?
- How did you show that you were a responsible citizen of the class today?
- Describe one negative emotion that you had to deal with in class today. How did you handle it?

Movement–Learning Connection

- Ask students to support their statements with facts.
- Have students give reasons for their comments.
- Allow students to reflect and use metacognition.
- Have students record how they refocused or helped the brain work as one.
- Have students apply the content of the question to out-of-school applications or to their future life.
- Read the students' work for content, not grammar or spelling.

Trex ⚛

NASPE Standards
1, 4, 6

Intelligence Types
N, K, IA

Thinking Skills
Variety, novelty, application, relating

Movement Skills
Locomotor and fitness exercises

Equipment
- Cards with names and pictures of trees or other content on them
- Pencils

Formation
Self-space

Description
1. Give each student a card with the name of a tree (a picture would be helpful) and ask him or her to come up with a fitness exercise that relates to (or can be associated with) that tree or some characteristic of that tree. For example, juniper could be associated with jumping (both start with the same letter), pine with rising and sinking motions (missing someone), and maple with running in place (like sap). The student then writes or draws the exercise to be performed on the back of the card, along with a number of repetitions.
2. Ask each student to provide a brief explanation of her or his association and demonstrate the actions.
3. Students then place their cards on the gym floor.
4. Ask students to "make like a tree and leave" their cards and go to another card.
5. When they come to another card, they read it and perform the exercises. When students finish one card, they move to another.

Movement–Learning Connection

- Play the game with another theme such as states, spelling words, or a body system.
- Have students come up with a variety of ways to associate movement with the word.
- Allow students to ask one peer for help if needed.
- Ask whether anyone has a question about the activity.
- Take students outdoors to identify trees.
- Include on the card two facts about the tree and have students read them as they are exercising.
- Develop a forest by calling all similar trees (e.g., fruit bearing) to group together. Have them perform a group activity like swaying as if they were blowing in the wind.

Collection Agency

NASPE Standards
1, 2, 5

Intelligence Types
K, IE

Thinking Skills
Comparison and contrast, classification, analysis

Movement Skills
Locomotor moves of choice, staying in a line

Equipment
Cards with criteria written on them

Formation
Five or more students designated as collectors, others scattered in general space

Description

1. Give five or more students, the collectors, cards that contain a *secret* characteristic common to some members of the class (e.g., wears glasses, is wearing light-colored shorts). Each card contains a different characteristic.

2. While the rest of the class is moving in general space, each collector tries to assemble as many fellow students as possible with the characteristic on the card by asking them to join his or her line. Upon finding someone with the characteristic the collector gently tags the person and asks, "Would you be so kind as to join my line?" The collected person replies, "Why thank you. I would be delighted to join your line."

3. The rest of the class continues to move in space until the collectors gather a sufficient number (or the whole class).

4. On the stop signal, each group gathers and attempts to determine the common characteristic. The noncollected students join a group to help.

5. When a group determines the correct answer and the leader verifies it, the group can try to guess the characteristic of the other groups.

6. Select a new group of collectors and give each a new card with a different characteristic on it.

Movement–Learning Connection

- Ask students how they figured out what the commonality was.
- Ask students to identify a characteristic that their group does not have in common.
- Ask what other characteristic the group has in common.
- Increase the characteristics to two per person.
- Make the characteristic subtler.
- Select characteristics that students would regard positively.
- Select the next collectors from those not selected for a group.
- Support positive communication.
- Have the group thank the collector for selecting them.

Movement Sentences

NASPE Standards
1, 2, 4

Intelligence Types
K, L, IE

Thinking Skills
Classification, composition, clarification

Movement Skills
Locomotor skills of choice

Equipment
Five to 10 hoops on the floor containing cards with words on them that form a sentence (e.g., We will run five laps to become aerobically fit!).

Formation
Individuals or small groups of two or three students moving in general space

Description
1. Direct students to move in general space from hoop to hoop using a particular locomotor skill.
2. When they come to a hoop, they turn one card over and attempt to make a sentence. If a sentence is not possible yet (not enough cards turned over), they move to the next hoop to turn a card over in that hoop.
3. When the last card is flipped, a sentence must be completed. The students gathered at the hoop read the sentence and perform the task.
4. The next students to come to the hoop (with the sentence already completed) perform the task and then move to the next hoop until all sentences are complete.

Movement–Learning Connection

- Have students identify the thinking skill that they are using (e.g., part–whole, synthesis).
- Send small groups of students to a hoop. Have them flip the cards, make the sentence, perform the task, and then flip and scramble the cards for the next group. When they finish, send them to another hoop.
- Ask the groups to make up a sentence to be used before the constructed sentence and another one to be used after the constructed sentence.
- Have students tell why the statement is factual.
- Ask why they think these statements are important in their lives.
- Have students contribute sentences.
- Leave blanks for students to fill in.
- Make the sentence more complex (e.g., We will run in place 15 steps at a fast pace, perform 30 crunches, and do 10 push-ups to become physically fit).

Centipede Challenge

NASPE Standards
2, 5

Intelligence Types
IE, K, N

Thinking Skills
Application, evaluation, problem solving, planning

Movement Skills
Group movement to complete task

Equipment
Large foam balls, beach balls, or soccer balls or volleyballs with some air removed so that they are soft and squishy; one for each student

Formations
Small groups, with three or four in a group

Description

1. Groups of three or four students form a centipede by placing balls between their bodies, thus joining themselves together. The first person in line holds a ball out in front as the head of the insect. Encourage students to select any arrangement that they think will work.

2. Each group moves from point A to point B without touching the balls with their hands or losing a ball. If they drop or touch a ball, the group must return to the start and try again.

3. After the group gets to point B, they can regroup (rearrange the balls), try a new formation, and then come back. Encourage students to try various alternatives and consider the opinions of all members of the group.

4. Emphasize completing the task, not competition. Choose a ball size that will challenge students and maintain safe body contact.

Movement–Learning Connection

- Ask students how they included the suggestions of group members.
- Have students change the structure into a different animal, such as a snake, crab, or imaginary creature.
- Add competition. Have a centipede race.
- Have students show the parts and then the whole (e.g., the people and ball are the parts, and the bug is the whole).
- Ask students whether they have ever seen a centipede.
- Teach about insects.
- Set up an obstacle course and have the centipedes move through it.

Clouds of Parachutes

NASPE Standards
5

Intelligence Types
N, K, S, IE

Thinking Skills
Identification, comparison and contrast, relating, problem solving

Movement Skills
Bending to move the parachute, movement to form shapes with the parachute

Equipment
As many parachutes as available

Formation
Parachutes with enough students around them to move them effectively

Description
1. Place students in groups around the parachutes.
2. Introduce types of clouds (e.g., cirrus, thunderhead). Show pictures and talk about cloud characteristics.
3. Give each group three minutes (longer if needed) to work out how they might use the parachute and their bodies to show the type of cloud in a safe way.
4. Allow the groups to try different possibilities. When a group is satisfied with their representation, give them another to work on.
5. At the end of class have students show their formations.

Movement–Learning Connection
- Have students build from a cumulus cloud into a thunderstorm.
- Ask how the shapes of clouds differ from one another.
- Ask each group how they used the input of all members of the group.
- Have students do contralateral exercises with the parachute.
- Have students show their work to another group to get feedback before they finish the task.
- Ask students what other weather conditions they could mimic with the parachute.
- After groups have determined their processes, call out the different types and give students a time limit to construct their clouds.
- Review weather safety.

Hoop-to-It Math

NASPE Standards
1, 2

Intelligence Types
LM, S, IE, K

Thinking Skills
Evaluation, reflection, planning

Equipment
Arrange hoops (or spots) of different colors in general space. Each color has a point value. For example, pink = 4, blue = 3, yellow = 2, and red = 1. In each hoop is a card with an exercise or skill written on it.

Formation
Mass or in smaller groups in separate sections of the space

Description
1. Tell or show students a number.
2. On a signal, students must go into (that is, place a foot in or jump into) the various colored hoops to reach the given number. Students add the points from each hoop that they touch until they reach the total. Students must touch two other hoops before they can touch the same hoop again.
3. When they reach the final hoop to make the total, students read the card in that hoop. Students perform the exercise in the hoop the number of times that matches the number of points that you asked them to accumulate.

Movement–Learning Connection
- Allow students some time to plot their course.
- Have students report the different combinations of numbers used.
- Have students set a goal and see whether they can make their goal (e.g., make the number in five hoops).
- Have students check each other's paths.
- Have students add aloud to assist you in monitoring their addition.
- Have students do the same activity but start with a number and subtract the points on the hoop until they reach zero. They perform the starting number of exercises for the exercise card in the last hoop.
- Give all students positive feedback.
- Have students work with partners, with one leading and the other checking (and helping).

Locomath `1+1=2`

NASPE Standards
1, 2, 5

Intelligence Types
LM, S, IE

Thinking Skills
Classification, recognizing patterns, clarification

Movement Skills
Various locomotor skills

Equipment
Various equipment of different colors or types

Formation
Small groups along a line with equipment strewn in general space

Description

1. Put students in groups of two or three and give each group a card with math questions and a code for the points that each item in general space is worth (e.g., red is worth 5 points or a hockey stick is worth 3 points). (See sample card on page 135.)

2. Each group works together to determine answers to the math problems.

3. Then, moving one at a time, they collect items whose point value, when added together, will equal the answer of the question on the sheet.

4. Check the answer. When it is correct, the group redistributes the equipment and goes on to the next problem.

5. To decrease competition, each group could have different questions and codes. For problems with higher value answers, students must collect an object that represents that number (e.g., hockey stick and red ball = 35 points).

Movement–Learning Connection

- Give students time to develop a plan.
- Ask students to share their strategies with another group.
- Ask students to repeat the problem with an alternative strategy. Have them explain which one worked best.
- If a group is having problems, have them do some contralateral exercises to get the whole brain working.
- Preview this activity by playing an activity in which students could learn the point values.
- Ask students to give positive feedback to each other.

Sample Locomath Card

1. $8 + 7 =$
2. $2 + 9 =$
3. $4 + 0 =$
4. $7 + 7 =$
5. $9 + 10 =$

Red hoop = 1 point
Basketball = 2 points
Green deck tennis ring = 3 points
Yellow hockey stick = 4 points
Juggling scarf = 5 points
Tennis ball = 6 points
Blue hoop = 7 points
Racket = 8 points
Jump rope = 9 points
Gymnastics mat = 10 points

The Best Meal

NASPE Standards
1, 5, 6

Intelligence Types
K, S, IE

Thinking Skills
Discernment, comparison and contrast, justification

Movement Skills
Locomotor skills as assigned

Equipment
- Names, pictures, or descriptions of a variety of foods placed on cards, or plastic foods
- One set of plastic dinner plates and spatulas for each group

Formation
Partners or small groups no larger than four along a line in relay formation, with foods scattered in general space

Description
1. Instruct students to develop the most nutritious meal from the selection available.
2. On the go signal, the first student in the group uses a designated locomotor skill to take the plate and spatula to the foods and select one. The student must use the spatula to handle the food and bring it back to the group on the plate. The second person goes next. Allow the group to consult or give instructions to teammates to help develop the meal.
3. When the teams have developed the best meals possible or have depleted the selection of foods, stop the game.
4. Ask each group to report on their meal and tell why it is or is not the best meal it could be.

Movement–Learning Connection
- Ask students to compare their meal with the meal of another group to determine which is the healthiest. Ask them to give reasons for their choice.

- Add a breakfast or lunch as a meal to find.
- Ask the groups why they chose the foods that they did.
- Give the groups a chart to figure the caloric value of the meals.
- Use other categories as items to collect such as healthy snacks, foods high in fat, or foods high in protein.
- Ask students to use only the spatula to transport the food. (Leave the plate back with the group.)
- Have students report on the healthiest meal that they ever ate in a restaurant.
- Have students tell how their favorite food makes them feel.
- Ask students to find a healthy vegetarian meal in the foods available.

Figure and Run

NASPE Standards
1, 5

Intelligence Types
K, LM, S, IE

Thinking Skills
Clarity, comparison and contrast, decision making, conditional reasoning

Movement Skills
Running or locomotor skills

Equipment
- Markers (e.g., cones, lines made of tape or chalk) to designate an area between the chasers and the taggers
- A line to run toward (to be safe) behind each group

Formation
Groups of three separated by a space of 3 to 8 feet (90 to 240 centimeters)

Description
1. Small groups of students set up opposite each other, behind the center marker. On a signal, students show an arbitrary number of fingers (one through five). Each group must add the number of fingers shown by the members of their group.
2. You then call out a characteristic to designate chasers (e.g., odd chases even, multiples of two are the chasers, the number closest to five are the chasers). If the number is the same (i.e., both groups are even) they do not run but wait for the next characteristic. If two groups are the same, the leader can give them an alternative characteristic.
3. On "Go," the designated chasers try to tag the members of the running team to add them to their side. Allow sufficient time for teams to add correctly. If the runners make it past the line into the safe zone without being tagged, they are safe.
4. After teams have the hang of the game, let students chase as soon as they figure out who the chasers are.

Movement–Learning Connection

- Ask students how they will be sure of their answer.
- Ask students if they have any questions.
- Ask students how they will add correctly when they are under the stress of deciding who is the chaser.
- Assign a different student to be the counter each time. Have the other students check his or her score.
- Keep the game moving so that all students are active.
- Have students suggest changes to the game.
- Teach the game in parts before putting it together.

Sentence Tag 📖

NASPE Standards
2, 5

Intelligence Types
L, K, S

Thinking Skills
Identification, ordering, recognizing patterns, problem solving

Movement Skills
Locomotor patterns

Equipment
- Sentence cards: Create sentences related to subjects that students are studying. Then put each word of the sentence on an individual card. Code the cards with colors so that it's clear which word cards go together to form a sentence. Make one or two cards to identify the chasers or "run-ons."
- Small dark-colored balls can be "periods."
- Items for the "run-ons" to carry to identify them as chasers (e.g., a foam ball the color of an eraser) or pinnies to wear.

Formation
General space. Tag game set up with color-coded areas marked as construction zones (e.g., a red cone for the red cards) placed outside the tag area. Place the color-coded cards with a single word of a sentence around the gym face down on the floor. For safety purposes, place the cards in specified areas or just outside the boundaries of the play area so that students do not step on them. Place the "erasers" and "periods" in a space on the floor away from each other and the construction areas. (See diagram on page 141.)

Description
1. Ask students to move in general space until you instruct them to pick up a card.
2. On your signal, students pick up a card. They have 20 seconds to read the word or identify themselves as a "run-on" or "period" by calling out their role and holding the card over their heads. If they are periods they pick up a ball. If they are chasers they can wear a pinny or carry an object identified as an eraser. Students with words move to the areas designated as sentence construction zones.

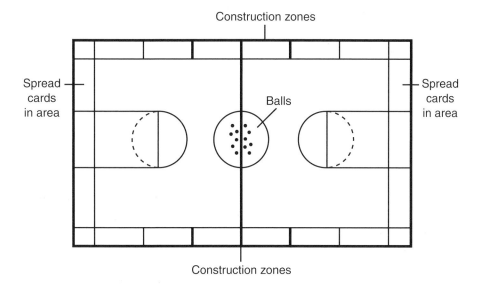

Construction zones

Spread cards in area

Balls

Spread cards in area

Construction zones

3. On a go signal, the students with the word cards gather by their colors in a construction zone and attempt to put their sentence together. Meanwhile the "run-ons" try to tag the "periods." If tagged, the period is erased and can't complete a sentence (he or she could become a tagger).

4. When they complete a sentence, students stand and line up in the correct order to complete a sentence. At this point, periods must try to complete the sentence by lining up at the end of the line of students. If the period is able to join a line, the sentence is complete. The group cheers and then sits down.

5. When all sentences are completed or you call time, the completed sentences perform a victory lap around the playing space.

6. The remaining students collect the cards and set up for the next game. At this point you could place a new set of cards with new sentences on the gym floor or redistribute the old set to play again. Instruct students to pick up a different colored card this time.

(continued)

Sentence Tag (continued)

Movement–Learning Connection

- To assist students in sentence construction, you could show sentences on an overhead projector or write them on a whiteboard.
- Start with sentences with simple structures and then make sentences more complex, depending on the abilities of the students.
- Let students practice with the same sentences a few times before changing the cards.
- Use facts that will have personal value for students.
- Review sentence structure before playing the game to assemble memories.
- Ask the periods to read the sentence and ask the run-ons to read the incomplete sentences before ending the game session.
- For the incomplete sentences ask students how they could complete the sentence to make sense.
- Ask students what strategy their color group used to figure out the sentence (e.g., the word that was capitalized was the first word; an adjective had to go with a noun).
- Use some of the sentences to preview future learning.

Food Fitness

NASPE Standards
4, 6

Intelligence Types
K, S, IE

Thinking Skills
Analysis, classification, application, identification

Movement Skills
Locomotor skills as assigned

Equipment
- Cards with pictures of foods or labels from food items on one side and an exercise on the other side
- A large poster of the food pyramid or a label from a food container

Formation
Mass in general space; cards are scattered on the floor

Description
1. On your signal, students move to a card, pick it up, and identify the type of food and what category on the food pyramid it fits into.
2. Before moving on to a new card, students must perform one exercise for each recommended daily serving allowance for that food. If you are using food labels, students perform one exercise for each percentage point of an ingredient (e.g., 5% saturated fat = 5 push-ups).

Movement–Learning Connection
- Ask students to make a judgment about a food from the label. Is the food essentially healthy or not healthy? They should give reasons for the judgment.
- Ask students to state aloud the daily recommended amount or the number of servings as they exercise.
- Have students tell the last time they ate that particular type of food.
- Ask students how they might use the information from the label in planning healthy meals.
- Ask why they should or should not (or why they would or would not) eat that particular food.

CHAPTER 6

Complex Activities

Island Survival

NASPE Standards

1, 2, 5, 6

Intelligence Types

K, LM, S, IE

Thinking Skills

Tolerance of ambiguity, evaluation, reflection, problem solving, decision making

Movement Skills

Various locomotor and nonlocomotor movements

Equipment

Jump ropes, cones, bases, deflated balls, hockey sticks, scooters, chairs, towels, mats, and so on

Formation

Groups of four or five arranged on "islands," or spaces designated in the area (e.g., the center circle on a basketball court). Each island has at least 10 items of various sizes and shapes. Have two unoccupied islands with equipment. The area around the islands is water and may not be traversed on foot. (See diagram on page 147.)

Description

1. Assemble each group and their equipment in a space designated as an island.
2. Instruct the groups that the object is to move the entire group and all the equipment across a space to another island. Students can move one at a time, or multiple students can move at once. The destination can be an island occupied by another group who will be moving onto another group's island, or you could move to an unoccupied island. Give students a few minutes to plot their strategy before starting. This event is not competitive. The activity ends when all the equipment and students are on a new island.
3. Rules:
   - Students may not throw any items from their islands except jump ropes.
   - Any student who touches the floor must return to the starting island.
   - If students get across to the destination island, they may come back (using equipment) to help others.

4. Ask students to evaluate their performance and develop ways in which they could cooperate or solve the problem more efficiently.
5. Then ask students to move their equipment and group members to another island.

Movement–Learning Connection

- Require students to use a problem-solving process.
- Be sure that each student has the opportunity to contribute his or her ideas.
- Allow students to try out a number of alternatives before starting "for real."
- After they complete the challenge once, ask the groups to solve the problem in a different way or come up with a better plan.
- Enforce positive consideration of the views of others.
- For a subsequent trial, change the roles of the group members, increase the distance that the groups must travel, or change the equipment available.
- Relate the activity to the students' lives. Ask where a situation like this could happen to them.
- If tension rises, have the group perform some deep-breathing exercises to reduce stress.
- For the next round use a scenario in which a volcano is about to erupt. Give students a reasonable number of minutes to complete the task before the volcano blows.

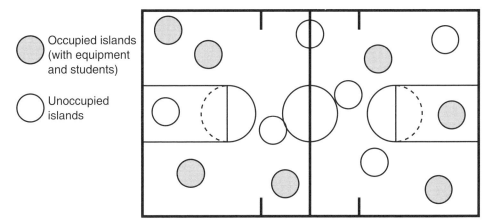

Occupied islands (with equipment and students)

Unoccupied islands

Survival Too

NASPE Standards

1, 2, 5

Intelligence Types

K, LM, S, IE

Thinking Skills

Tolerance of ambiguity, planning, evaluation, illustration

Movement Skills

Various moves to complete the task

Equipment

A variety of equipment available in one area

Formation

Islands where groups gather to begin are located throughout the gym. In one space a selection of equipment is available. (See diagram on page 149.)

Description

1. Each student, before the start of the lesson, selects one piece of equipment. Do not tell students why they are making a choice.

2. After the groups assemble with their equipment, give them the assignment to vacate their present island to move to another island, taking all group members and possessions with them.

3. Ask students to suggest the rules of play, such as the following:
   - Only one person at a time can be on a single piece of equipment on the "water."
   - Equipment may not be thrown except for the ropes.
   - Students may not skate or ski or slide across the space.
   - If one person touches the "water," the whole group must go back and start again.

4. When a group reaches a destination, assign them a new destination. Allow the group to trade in two pieces of equipment for two new pieces.

Movement–Learning Connection

- Ask what the equipment they chose could be used for in this task.
- Ask what one piece of equipment they wish they had.
- Ask how they evaluated the success of each attempt.
- Ask students what they learned.
- Have groups cheer a successful crossing.
- Allow groups to trade equipment.
- Ask each group what they are willing to trade to get other equipment from you or another group (payment in exercise or other item).
- Have students do exercises to warm up their brains before starting.
- Allow a group that has successfully reached an island where another group is having problems making a successful crossing to join the second group, combine their equipment, and try again.
- Require that all group members contribute.

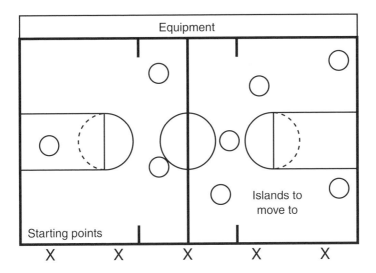

Personal Warm-Up

NASPE Standards
2, 3, 4, 5

Intelligence Types
IA, K, LM

Thinking Skills
Goal setting, planning, evaluation

Movement Skills
Exercises or skills being taught

Equipment
- Paper and pencil to record list of moves for a task goal
- List of potential moves posted for all to see

Formation
General space with areas set up for tasks to be completed

Description
1. When students enter the gymnasium, give each a pencil and paper and ask them to make a list of the exercises that they will perform as a personal warm-up. Encourage students to draw pictures and describe the exercises in words. You may need to review the components of a good warm-up.
2. Ask students to develop their warm-ups so that they directly relate to the activity of the day (e.g., running the mile or playing tag games).
3. You can assign the number of exercises that they must list and the number of repetitions for each exercise, or you can allow them to decide.
4. When they complete the written work, each student must complete his or her personal warm-up individually.
5. When they finish, students report to an area and begin participation in a class activity until all students have completed their warm-ups.

Movement–Learning Connection

- Ask students to assess how their warm-up prepared them for the activity of the day (or their personal goals).
- Discuss the procedure students used to decide which exercises to include.
- Have students read the instructions for the activity on the board or on the sheet of paper rather than give the instructions orally.
- Start class from a different spot than usual (e.g., in the center of the gym).
- Ask students to share their warm-ups with a partner for the next class.

Personal Assessment

NASPE Standards
2, 3, 4, 6

Intelligence Types
IA, K, L

Thinking Skills
Goal setting, planning, evaluation, reflection

Movement Skills
Depends on the skills, routines, or performance to be assessed

Equipment
Pencils and an assessment form (see table 6.1, page 153, for a sample)

Formation
Self-space

Description

1. After a performance or skill instruction, ask students to assess their performance based on the criteria that you supply. The assessment tool could be a form or just a sheet of paper on which students write their reflections.

2. Ask students to suggest ways in which they could improve their performance.

3. Ask students to develop two activities that they could perform during the next class that would help them improve.

4. Allow time in the next class for students to practice their activities.

Movement–Learning Connection

- Ask students whether they feel that their assessment truly represents their fitness or effort.

- Allow students to discuss and share techniques to improve their motivation, skill, or fitness.

- Have students develop a goal for the next assessment.
- Have students justify their rating with reasons.
- Allow students to assess each other.
- Have students build a reward into their plans.
- Support improvements in student fitness or skill levels.
- Allow students the opportunity to reassess themselves later.

Table 6.1 Assessment Rubric: Free Throw

Criteria	Yes	Not yet	Helpful comments
Feet still			
Eyes on basket			
Same warm-up routine every time			
Moderate knee bend			
Smooth extension of legs			
Followed by extension of arms			
High follow-through with arms			
Fingertips point toward basket			

Sport Shop

NASPE Standards
1, 2, 5

Intelligence Types
K, IE, LM

Thinking Skills
Justification, classification, planning, view from a variety of perspectives

Movement Skills
Locomotor movement of choice

Equipment
One hoop for each group for their store and one hoop for each supplier. Within the several supplier hoops should be three to eight items of at least 10 different pieces of equipment. Items should be mixed in the supplier hoops, not grouped together.

Formation
Five or fewer in each group. Place hoops in the gym to represent stores. The stores could be set up as a strip mall (in a line) with the goods or suppliers in an area across from the hoops or as a megamall (in a large circle) with the goods in the center of the circle. Place hoops with a variety of equipment at a variety of distances (if possible) from the stores. (See diagram on page 155.)

Description
1. Tell each group that they are buyers for a sporting goods store. Their job is to corner the market on a particular type of sporting good by collecting at least six of any one item.

2. Before play, give the groups a few minutes to plot their strategy. Besides collecting six of one item for themselves, they need to consider how they will stop others from collecting six of one item.

3. On the signal to start, the first shopper, holding a deck tennis ring (credit card) to identify herself or himself, goes to one of the hoops and picks up one item. The shopper takes the item back to the group and places it in the group's store (hoop).

4. The first shopper hands off the ring (credit card) to the next person, who goes to select another or the same item. Shoppers from each group collect items as fast as they can, one at a time. Warn shoppers to be careful when carrying equipment and to watch out for other shoppers.

5. Stop the game after a few minutes. Each group that has collected six items of a particular type gets 1 point.

6. Reset the game and allow time for groups to plot a new strategy or plan.

Movement–Learning Connection

- Ask students if they had any problems. Ask how they could handle them in the next game.
- Ask students to evaluate the new plan.
- Have the groups share their strategies.
- Change the scoring of the game. Groups score 1 point for having the most of an item or for having the most varied collection.
- Allow each group time to make up their own collection goals.
- Give some items higher point values (to increase the demand).
- Use tax collectors in the space between the hoops and the stores. If a tax collector tags a shopper, the group has to give up one item to the tax collector, who places it back in supply.
- After the game has ended, allow the groups two minutes to barter or exchange equipment between groups. Then award points.

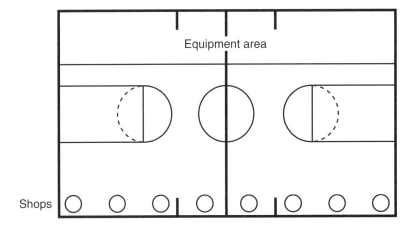

Mediator in Training

NASPE Standards
5

Intelligence Types
IE, IA

Thinking Skills
Objective observation, analysis, view from a variety of perspectives, decision making, problem solving, application

Movement Skills
Nonlocomotor skills, skills relating to the movement setting on the card

Equipment
- Markers for mediation stations
- Posters stating the mediation process
- Sports equipment as necessary to act out the scenarios

Formation
Small groups of two to four, five or six mediation stations with a student and a chart with the process of mediation to be used written on it

Description
Use this activity as a break for students during activity. At a natural pause in a game or activity (e.g., time-out or change of teams), call the groups together and distribute the cards. Before this activity, students should have received an introduction to the mediation process that is used with this activity.

1. Give each group a card. One card is the mediation card. Members of the group that receives this card go to the mediation centers on the perimeter and review the mediation process.
2. The other groups will receive conflict scenario cards. These cards will have on them a description of a conflict situation common in movement settings. These groups gather their equipment and practice acting out the scenario. All students in the group must be involved in the skit.
3. On a signal the scenario groups go to a mediation station and act out their conflict in front of a mediator.

4. As the conflict unfolds, the mediator intervenes appropriately using the conflict resolution process posted on the wall. After the situation plays itself out, the scenario group gives feedback to the mediator on the conflict resolution process.

5. Groups return to play until you start the next mediator in training exercise by redistributing the cards to the groups.

Movement–Learning Connection

- Encourage and model effective communication skills.
- Have mediators assess their performance after receiving feedback from the scenario group.
- Ask students to develop their own scenarios.
- Use conflicts that relate to students on a personal level.
- Stress the benefits of win–win negotiations.
- Use a stress-reduction technique if emotion rises.

Personal Pattern Moves

NASPE Standards
2, 4

Intelligence Types
LM, S, IE

Thinking Skills
Planning, problem solving, identification, evaluation

Movement Skills
Running or whatever locomotor pattern you choose

Equipment
- A series of cones or spots set up in a grid with 6 to 10 feet (2 to 3 meters) between each marker. Mark the cones 0 to 10 (or however large) on the *x* and *y* axes.
- Cards with a path or a shape on them

Formation
Individuals or pairs of students, standing behind a line facing the grid

Description
1. Each student receives a card with a path or shape on it with dots marking specific points that are located in relation to their position on the *x* and *y* axes. (See sample card on page 159.) The student must replicate the shape on the card by jogging to the points on the grid.
2. On the second run, ask students to identify the coordinates for each point by recording them in order on the back of the card (e.g., 4, 9).
3. Group students with partners. One partner shows his or her pathway and then checks the partner's path by using the coordinates previously written on the back of the card. The partner should walk or run the pathway.

Movement–Learning Connection

- Allow students to draw the coordinates on graph paper before they run.
- Students could call out the coordinates to their partners.
- Ask students to be as accurate as possible.
- Ask groups to exchange cards with other groups to try other paths.
- For variety have each student make up a set of coordinates.
- Have students identify the patterns that their paths or coordinates formed (e.g., square).
- Two students could combine lists of coordinates and run through them in order.

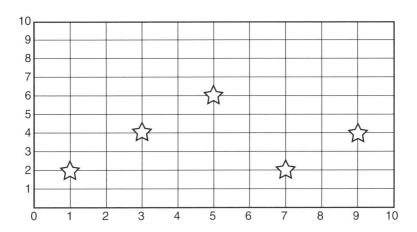

Instant Replay

NASPE Standards
2, 5

Intelligence Types
IE, K, S

Thinking Skills
Decision making, problem solving, reflection, evaluation

Movement Skills
Movement skills necessary to play the game when instant replay is requested

Equipment
As needed to play a game

Formation
As needed for the team, with a student designated to ask for an instant replay

Description
Use this activity during a scrimmage or game.

1. During any game, a designated team member may request an instant replay after a game incident (e.g., a foul committed, an interception, a score). You may choose to also be designated to call for an instant replay.

2. The team must reset the situation as it was before the incident and then replay the game from that point exactly as it happened. Both teams now have the opportunity to see where they could make adjustments to support team play in similar situations. You could suggest other strategies or ways in which they might handle the situation. You can determine the number of instant replays allowed in a game. Begin with two or three per game.

3. After seeing the alternatives to a situation, reset the game and restart it from the point before the incident.

Movement–Learning Connection

- Ask the team who called the replay to gather and plan a strategy to change the course of the original play. The opponents must start the play but can adjust to their opponent's new strategy.
- Ask how the second attempt was better or worse than the first.
- Perform the replay in slow motion as it is or as adjusted.
- Teams could use the instant replay to question or understand a call by the official.
- Have teams give reasons for success or failure.
- Have both teams perform some contralateral movements to ready the brain for the restart.
- The real-life drama will focus students on the game and its strategies.
- Use the moment to teach about reducing the stress generated by the replay act.

Make a Play

NASPE Standards
2, 5

Intelligence Types
IE, S

Thinking Skills
Analysis, synthesis, problem solving

Movement Skills
Running, pathways

Equipment
Sports equipment for the sport being taught at the time

Formation
Groups around the space available (field, gymnasium)

Description
1. Give groups a problem of developing a play or strategy for the game that they are learning (e.g., inbounding a ball over a sideline, developing a pattern of team movement to produce an attempt to score, defending a goal, or getting open to receive a pass). Give them time to design, diagram, and practice a workable play for the given situation.
2. Ask students to show their plays to each other and allow the designers to coach the other groups through the execution of the play.
3. The groups who are learning the plays can give feedback to the designers, which they can use to perfect the play.
4. When students play the game, require the groups to use the plays and strategies that they learned in this activity.

Movement–Learning Connection
- Use the task to develop respectful communication between students.
- Ask the group to outline the process that they used to develop the play.
- When practicing the play, players should vary their speed, space, and positions.
- Have groups try the plays against other groups.

Circuit Setup

NASPE Standards
1, 2, 5

Intelligence Types
IE, K, S, L

Thinking Skills
Problem solving, goal setting, illustration, recalling

Movement Skills
Movement skills as necessary to complete the station tasks

Equipment
Whatever is necessary for students to work efficiently at the stations

Formation
Small groups scattered in general space

Description
1. Assign groups of three to areas in the gym to develop movement stations. Each group must design a station to meet a particular instructional goal or objective. For example, the objective of a station could be to improve dribbling a basketball without looking at the ball. Students then come up with a way to practice dribbling without looking at the ball. The station must be active and promote quality practice opportunities, and its design must allow all students to be successful.
2. After students develop the activity, ask them to assemble the necessary equipment and practice the station to be sure that it is workable.
3. Ask students to produce a poster describing the activity at the station. A small whiteboard works well for this.
4. Ask students to develop a rotation system and have them rotate from station to station to practice their skills.

Movement–Learning Connection
- Give students a worksheet to help them meet their goals.
- Ask students to give feedback on the stations. Before they rotate and practice at all the stations, have each group try another group's station and give the designers feedback.
- Ask students to evaluate the success of their stations. Ask whether they need to make changes.
- Include a relaxation station or a station to refocus the brain with appropriate exercises.
- Ask students why development of their particular skill will improve their performance of the game or activity.

Robot ⚛

NASPE Standards
1, 2, 5, 6

Intelligence Types
K, S, IA, IE

Thinking Skills
Objective observation, recalling, decision making

Movement Skills
Walking, jogging

Equipment
Obstacles to place in the environment

Formation
Pairs in general space

Description

1. Place students in pairs. One of the pair is a robot operator, and the other is the robot.

2. Ask the pairs to figure out what signals they will use to direct the robot, who is without sight (eyes closed). The operator must give the signals by appropriate touching. Ask students to decide how to signal movement forward, movement backward, and turns to the right and left. They also need signals to stop and start, and they may choose to develop other signals. To begin, or with younger students, designate the commands ahead of time (e.g., touch right shoulder = do a half turn to the right, tap middle of back = stop).

3. The pairs decide who will be the robot and who will be the operator. The operator and robot practice the signals in general space.

4. Allow the pairs to switch roles. Then have the pairs try the signals on an obstacle course.

Movement–Learning Connection

- Change the robots' abilities so that they can see but not hear. The signals now must be visual.
- Ask students to change their signals from touch to auditory. Ask which method works better.
- Add another robot to each group so that the operator must control two robots.
- Ask students how they will remember the signals.
- Ask students how the operator will keep the robot safe.
- Show off the robots in a competition.
- Ask students how it felt to be in charge and to be dependent.

Tag Team Fitness

NASPE Standards

1, 2, 4

Intelligence Types

K, S

Thinking Skills

Problem solving, decision making, planning, goal setting

Movement Skills

A variety of fitness activities

Equipment

- Mats
- Fitness apparatus
- Clear path for running
- A list of possible fitness exercises or activities

Formation

Areas set up for a variety of fitness exercises, groups of three students

Description

1. Assemble groups of three students. Each group can be composed of students who have different fitness levels. The group is made up of the exerciser, the on-deck exerciser, and the coach or third exerciser. The goal for each group is to complete as many repetitions of the selected exercise as possible in a specified time limit. Start with one minute.

2. Ask each team to select 10 exercises from the list provided to address the five areas of fitness (at least one exercise must address each fitness component). You could decide on the exercises ahead of time and assign them to the teams.

3. Each team must set a team performance goal for each exercise that they have selected. They also decide who will start each exercise bout and the subsequent order of who will follow whom, keeping in mind the performance goal.

4. When the groups are ready, start the clock. The exerciser begins the exercise, and the coach counts the repetitions and monitors the exerciser until he or she breaks form (no longer performs the exercise correctly) or begins to exhibit a decline in performance.

5. At this point the coach instructs the on-deck exerciser to tag the current performer and take over performance of the exercise. The replaced exerciser becomes the coach and continues the count. The replaced coach is now on deck to exercise next. Team members continue to exchange roles until you call time.

6. Ask students to assess whether they met their goal.

Movement–Learning Connection

- Ask students to list a number of ways in which they can motivate their peers.
- Have groups give a rationale for the exercises that they chose.
- Have students record their performance and then compare performances over a period of time.
- Ask groups who met their goal to give each other a high 10 to celebrate their accomplishment. Then ask them to set a new goal.
- Ask groups what strategies they used to make or beat their goal.
- Ask each member of the group which fitness area is most important to him or her.
- Ask whether working alone or in a group is better for each individual.

Sport Skills Square Dance

NASPE Standards

1, 2, 5, 6

Intelligence Types

M, K, IE, S, L

Thinking Skills

Recalling, application, composition, problem solving, elaboration

Movement Skills

Any sports skills, basic square dance formations and moves

Equipment

- CD player
- Square dance music without words

Formation

Square dance formation (four sets of partners), initial planning groups of three to five students

Description

1. Ask students to listen to a square dance song without the caller. Review the components of square dance by having the groups perform a simple dance.

2. Tell students that rather than square dance they are going to make up a sport square dance using the skills of the sport or movement that they have just studied (e.g., gymnastics, baseball) in combination with traditional square dance moves. For example, with the sport of baseball, groups could perform the following dance:

   - "Circle right" could become "run around the bases to your right until you get home."
   - They could do a "do-si-do" by moving around each other in the position that they would hold for a bunt.
   - "Head couples up to the middle and back" could become "head couples up to the middle and bat" in which the head couples move into the center and pretend to swing a bat.

3. The group must assemble the dance and develop the calls to go with it. One of the students takes the role of the caller and performs that role when the group presents or teaches the dance to the rest of the class.

Movement–Learning Connection

- Ask students how they will decide what moves fit the music.
- Ask students how they incorporated the views of all members of their group.
- Have students explain how they solved the problem.
- Ask students how they decided on one move over another.
- Show an example of a sport dance.
- Ask students if they recognize dance steps in sport and sport skills in dance.
- Allow time for development and practice.

Current Events

NASPE Standards
2, 5, 6

Intelligence Types
IE, IA, K

Thinking Skills
Analysis, problem solving, reflection, synthesis

Movement Skills
As needed

Equipment
Space to work

Formation
Groups of three to five

Description

1. Have each group identify (or give them) a current event (e.g., a fire in a downtown building, a bad weather situation, or an upcoming school celebration).
2. Each student gives her or his impressions of the event to the group.
3. When all students have contributed, the group considers the contributions of each student as they develop a movement sequence that illustrates the group's combined thoughts and feelings about the event.
4. The movement sequence must have a beginning, middle, and end. The groups may choose to break down the event into components or parts, and report or mimic the event. Older students can be more abstract and develop a dance in which they use concepts, emotions, and themes to develop the essence of the event.
5. Each group could present their movement sequence to the class.

Movement–Learning Connection

- Ask each member to write a before and after impression of the original event.
- Ask the viewers to discuss or write how the acts affected them.
- Ask students how they came to a decision about what to include or not include in their sequence.
- Encourage students to end the movement series on a hopeful or positive note.
- Help students deal with emotions.

Musical Setup

NASPE Standards
1, 2, 5

Intelligence Types
S, M, IE, K

Thinking Skills
Recalling, composition, application

Movement Skills
Locomotor patterns

Equipment
CD player

Formation
Students move in general space to music, with a space designated for the setup. Have enough spaces so that all students can be part of a setup.

Description
1. Assign students to groups according to the number needed to set up or start any game, team, or movement formation. For example, for volleyball use groups of six and for dance use groups of eight. Assign each group an area in which to set up.
2. Play music and have groups separate and move in general space until the music stops.
3. At the signal they move to their assigned area and set up the formation that you request (e.g., serve reception in volleyball, two by two in line of direction in dance).

Movement–Learning Connection
- Ask students to self-assess the group response.
- Ask students to generalize their performance on a scale of 1 to 5, from "great" to "needs work."
- Have each group meet after the fact to figure out a better response to the next assignment.
- Use a countdown to move the activity along.
- Raise the emotion level by giving points for the fastest response.
- Relate this activity to what needs to happen when students actually play a game.

REFERENCES

Armstrong, T. 2000. *Multiple intelligences in the classroom.* Alexandria, VA: Association for Supervision and Curriculum Development.

Baron, J.B. 1986. Evaluating thinking skills in the classroom. In *Teaching thinking skills: Theory and practice,* ed. J.B. Baron and R.J. Sternburg. New York: W.H. Freeman.

Beyer, B. 1987. *Practical strategies for the teaching of thinking.* Boston: Allyn and Bacon.

Blakemore, C.L. 2003. Movement is essential to learning. *Journal of Physical Education, Recreation and Dance* 74(9):22-28, 41.

Blitzer, L. 1995. It's a gym class . . .What's there to think about? *Journal of Physical Education, Recreation and Dance* 6(6):44-48.

Bloom, B., ed. 1956. *Taxonomy of educational objectives.* New York: Longmans.

Bransford, J.D., R.D. Sherwood, and T. Sturdevant. 1986. Teaching, thinking and problem solving. In *Teaching thinking skills: Theory and practice,* ed. J.B. Baron and R.J. Sternburg. New York: W.H. Freeman.

Brink, S. May 15, 1995. Smart moves: New presence suggests that folks from 8-80 can shape up their brains with aerobic exercise. *U.S. News & World Report* (online database), pp. 78-82.

Bruer, J.T. 1991. The brain and child development: Time for some critical thinking. *Public Health Reports* 113(5):388-97.

Buell, C., and A. Whittaker. 2001. Enhancing content literacy in physical education. *Journal of Health, Physical Education, Recreation and Dance* 72(6):32-37.

Buschner, C.A. 1990. Can we help children move and think critically? In *Moving and learning for the young child,* ed. W.S. Stinson. Reston, VA: AAHPERD.

Choo, L.H., and P.D. Jewel. 2001. Martial arts and critical thinking in the gifted education curriculum. *Talent Education* 19(1):15.

Costa, A.L., and R. Garmson. 1991. *The school as a home for the mind: A collection of articles,* ed. A.L. Costa. Thousand Oaks, CA: Corwin Press.

Dennison, P.E., and G. Dennison. 1986. *Brain gym, simple activities for whole brain learning.* Ventura, CA: Edu-Kinesthetics.

Dennison, P.E., and G. Dennison. 1988. *Brain gym, teachers edition.* Ventura, CA: Edu-Kinesthetics.

Diamond, M., and J. Hopson. 1998. *Magic trees of the mind: How to nurture your child's intelligence, creativity and healthy emotions from birth through adolescence.* New York: Dutton Books, Penguin-Putnam Group.

Ennis, C.D. 1991. Discrete thinking skills in two teachers' physical education classes. *Elementary School Journal* 91(5):473-87.

Ennis, R.H. 1986. A taxonomy of critical thinking dispositions and abilities. In *Teaching thinking skills: Theory and practice,* ed. J.B. Baron and R.J. Sternburg. New York: W.H. Freeman.

Ennis, R. 2000a. A super-streamlined conception of critical thinking. www.criticalthinking.net/SSConcCTApr3.html.

Ennis, R. 2000b. Teaching critical thinking: A few suggestions. Available at www.criticalthinking.net/teaching.html.

Fowler, B. 1996. Bloom's taxonomy and critical thinking. *Critical thinking across the curriculum project.* Lee's Summit, MO: Longview Community College.

Freeland, K. 1995. Become a good example, modeling critical thinking behavior in physical education. *Teaching High School Physical Education* October:6-7.

Gardner, H. 1993. *Frames of mind: The theory of multiple intelligences.* New York: Basic Books.

Gerney, P.E. 1993. Teaching critical thinking (a practical approach). Paper presented at the American Alliance for Health, Physical Education, Recreation and Dance National Convention and Exposition, Washington, DC, March 25.

Hannaford, C. 1995. *Smart moves: Why learning is not all in your head.* Marshall, NC: Great Ocean.

Hinson, C. 1995. *Fitness for children.* Champaign, IL: Human Kinetics.

Jensen, E. 1998a. *Introduction to brain compatible learning.* San Diego: The Brain Store.

Jensen, E. 1998b. *Teaching with the brain in mind.* Alexandria, VA: Association for Supervision and Curriculum Development.

Jensen, E. 2000. Moving with the brain in mind. *Educational Leadership* November:34-37.

Johnson, R. 1997. Question techniques to use in teaching. *Journal of Physical Education, Recreation and Dance* 68(8):45-49

Kamla, J., and J. Lindaur. 2002. Integrating critical thinking strategies in physical education. *Strategies* 16(2):27-29.

Kempermann, G., Kuhn, H.G., and Gage, F. 1997. More hippocampal neurons in adult mice living in an enriched environment. *Nature* 38: 493-95.

Kinoshita, H. 1997. Run for your brain's life. *Brain-work* 7(1):8.

Martens, F. 1982. Daily physical education a boon to Canadian elementary schools. *Journal of Physical Education, Recreation and Dance* 53(3): 55-58.

McBride, R.E. 1989. Teaching critical thinking on the psychomotor learning environment: A possibility of a passing phase? *The Physical Educator* 46:170-72.

McBride, R.E. 1992. Critical thinking—An overview with implications for physical education. *Journal of Teaching in Physical Education* 11:112-15.

McBride, R.E. 1995. Critical thinking—An idea whose time has come. *Journal of Physical Education, Recreation and Dance* 66(6):22-23.

McBride, R.E. 1999. If you structure it they will learn it: Critical thinking in physical education classes. *Clearing House* 72(4):217-21.

McBride, R.E., and R. Bonnette. 1995. Teacher and at-risk students' cognition during open-ended activities: Structuring the learning environment for critical thinking. *Teaching and Teacher Education* 11:373-88.

Michaud, E. and R. Wilde. 1991. *Boost your brain power.* Emmaus, PA: Rodale Press.

Nash, M.J. 1997. Fertile minds. *Time* 149(5):48-56.

National Association for Sport and Physical Education (NASPE). 2004. *Moving into the future: National standards for physical education.* 2nd ed. Reston, VA: AAHPERD.

Nickerson, R. 1986. Why teach thinking? In *Teaching thinking skills: Theory and practice,* ed. J.B. Baron and R.J. Sternburg. New York: W.H. Freeman.

Norris, S., and R. Ennis. 1989. *Evaluating critical thinking.* Pacific Grove, CA: Midwest Publications Critical Thinking Press.

Ocansey, R. 1994. Planning high school physical education lessons to encourage critical thinking. *ICHPER-SD Journal* Winter:16-21.

Paul, R. 1992. *Critical thinking, what every person needs to survive in a rapidly changing world.* 2nd ed. Santa Rosa, CA: Foundation for Critical Thinking.

Perkins, D.N. 1986. Thinking frames: An integrative perspective on teaching cognitive skills. In *Teaching thinking skills: Theory and practice,* ed. J.B. Baron and R.J. Sternburg. New York: W.H. Freeman.

Piaget, J. 1963. *The origins of intelligence.* New York: Norton.

Placek, J.O., and M. Sullivan. 1997. The many faces of integrated physical education. *Journal of Physical Education, Recreation and Dance* 68(1):20-24.

Potts, B. 1994. *Strategies for teaching critical thinking.* ERIC clearinghouse on assessment and evaluation. ED 385606.

Promislow, S. 1999. *Making the brain–body connection: A playful guide to releasing mental, physical and emotional blocks to success.* Vancouver, BC, Canada: Kinetic.

Quellmalz, E.S. 1986. Developing reasoning skills. In *Teaching thinking skills: Theory and practice,* ed. J.B. Baron and R.J. Sternburg. New York: W.H. Freeman.

Rovengno, I., R. Skonie, T. Charpenel, and J. Sieving. 1995. Learning to teach critical thinking through child-centered games. *Journal of Physical Education, Recreation and Dance* 64(5):1-15.

Ruggiero, V.R. 1985. *The art of thinking: A guide to critical and creative thought.* New York: HarperCollins.

Savoy, G. 1971. *Archery—A catalyst for subject integration.* ERIC. ED 085149 RC 007494.

Schwager, S., and C. Labate. 1993. Teaching for critical thinking in physical education. *Journal of Physical Education, Recreation and Dance* 64(5):24-26.

Sherman, C.P. 1999. Integrating mental management skills into the physical education curriculum. *Journal of Physical Education, Recreation and Dance* 70(5):25-30.

Silverman, S. 1993. Student characteristics, practice and achievement in physical education. *Journal of Educational Research* 87(1):54-61.

Skon, L., D.W. Johnson, and R.T. Johnson. 1981. Cooperative peer interaction versus individual competition and individualistic efforts: Effects on the acquisition of cognitive reasoning strategies. *Journal of Education Psychology* 73(1):83-92.

Sternburg, R.J. 1983. *How can we teach intelligence?* Philadelphia: Research for Better Schools.

Stillman, L. 1989. Handling stress through stretching. In *Critical thinking handbook: High school, a guide for redesigning instruction,* ed. R. Paul, A.J.A. Binker, D. Martin, and K. Adamson. Santa Rosa, CA: Foundation for Critical Thinking.

Swartz, R.J. 1986. Restructuring curriculum for critical thinking. *Educational Leadership* May:43-44.

Swartz, R.J., and D.N. Perkins. 1990. *Teaching thinking: Issues and approaches.* Pacific Grove, CA: Midwest.

Tishman, S., and D.N. Perkins. 1995. Critical thinking and physical education. *Journal of Physical Education, Recreation and Dance* 66(6):24-33.

Werner, P. 1995. Moving out of the comfort zone to address critical thinking. *Teaching Elementary Physical Education* October: 6, 7, 9.

West, J. 1989. Soccer tactics. In *Critical thinking handbook: High school, a guide for redesigning instruction,* ed. R. Paul, A.J.A. Binker, D. Martin, and K. Adamson. Santa Rosa, CA: Foundation for Critical Thinking.

Wolfe, P. 2001. *Brain matters, translating research into classroom practice.* Alexandria, VA: Association for Supervision and Curriculum Development.

Woods, A.M., and C. Bok. 1995. Critical thinking in middle school physical education. *Journal of Physical Education, Recreation and Dance* August: 39-43.

ABOUT THE AUTHOR

Mary E. Clancy, PhD, has been teaching for more than 30 years. An associate professor and coordinator of the physical education teacher education program in the department of exercise and sport studies at the University of Tampa, Clancy has studied the thinking and brain-friendly development processes, developed a model to assist in the development of thinking, and made numerous presentations on related topics. A lover of movement and activity, she sees movement as the perfect vehicle to help children learn to think, be successful in their daily lives, make healthy decisions, and become independent.